BECOMING THE RIPPLE

YOUR GUIDE TO EXPONENTIALLY INCREASING YOUR PROFESSIONAL SUCCESS AND INFLUENCE

DAPHNE VALCIN

Becoming the Ripple
By Daphne Valcin
Copyright © 2024 Valcin Strategic Solutions

Cover Design: Tri Widyatmaka
Cover Photography: LNJ Designs/ Leslie Jean-Goins

If you would like to purchase bulk copies of Becoming the Ripple, contact us at info@valcinsolutions.com for discount pricing.

First edition, September 2024

ISBN-13: 979-8-9914820-0-4

Printed in the United States of America

All rights reserved. This book or any portion thereof may not be reproduced or used in any manner whatsoever without the express written permission of the publisher except for the use of brief quotations in a book review.

DEDICATION

To my two little girls, Jasmine and Gabrielle. I hope you someday are "becoming the ripple" both personally and professionally, in a way that surpasses your dreams and inspires others.

ACKNOWLEDGMENTS

I am grateful to Tammy Way, who urged me to write a book and helped me understand how powerful it could be to serve others through my writing. I thank Geovanni Derice, my book coach, for helping me with every step of my book writing and publishing process. I thank my husband, Bobby, and my children, Gabrielle and Jasmine, for their patience and support as I wrote this book. And a huge thank you to the leaders and organizations who have given me the honor of supporting and equipping them toward their vision and dreams. I am inspired by every one of you and count it a privilege to have served you.

Contents

Part I – Your Why 1
    Chapter 1 – Your "Why" Will Push You Further Faster 3
    Chapter 2 – Put Your Why in Front of You 11
    Chapter 3 – Stay Ready 17

Part II – Your Action 25
    Chapter 4 – Explore What Truly Matters 27
    Chapter 5 – Practice Targeted Time 35
    Chapter 6 – Use the Rule of 3s 43

Part III – Your Voice 47
    Chapter 7 – Remember Your 3 Keys 49
    Chapter 8 – Be Who You Aspire to Be 57
    Chapter 9 – Analyze Your Tone 63

Part IV – Your Environment 71
    Chapter 10 – Be a Culture Changer 73
    Chapter 11 – Implement the "One-thing" Principle 81
    Chapter 12 – Be the Change You Want to See 85

Part V – Your Special Touch 93
    Chapter 13 – Identify Your Special Sauce 95
    Chapter 14 – Infuse Your Strengths Into Your Work 101
    Chapter 15 – Becoming the Ripple: Making W.A.V.E.S.™ 107

Afterword 113

PART I

YOUR WHY

CHAPTER 1

Your "Why" Will Push You Further Faster

"Whatever you can do, or dream you can, begin it. Boldness has genius, power, and magic in it." – Johann Wolfgang von Goethe

Can you recall a time when you heard of someone doing something that defied the odds? Maybe it made you ask yourself with admiration, "How could they have done *all* of *that*?" Every day, professionals worldwide live lives that defy the odds they have been given. People get promoted into positions others have said they were not qualified for. People take on projects and exceed expectations despite being newer in their roles or having a team with limited capacity. People show up and speak up at work in a way they never imagined they would based on some aspects of their childhoods. People attain new roles within different departments at work that are such a dream to them that in the days leading up to their first day in their role, they still can't believe the opportunity is real.

This book, "Becoming the Ripple," was written as a result of my working with over 400 individual clients and over 200 organizational clients for more than ten years through coaching, consulting, training, and program development and witnessing what causes the greatest success in individuals and companies, and what can hinder progress.

What I have witnessed in my work is that when individuals operate fully within their potential, exceeding expectations, feeling fully aligned with their work, and pushing past challenges, it creates a ripple effect. Teams are impacted, companies are impacted, and even the personal lives of those individuals are impacted. However, what's different about those who create this ripple effect is that they are continuously creating the ripple–in essence, they are becoming the ripple. Their commitment to growth and excellence is ongoing, even as their priorities, roles, or capacity change. I hope this book inspires you, equips you, helps you think differently about something that could impact you personally or professionally, or adds new perspectives to your journey as you strive for success.

In the following pages, I'll use my signature WAVES™ framework for how to grow your influence and impact to expound on what it can look like for you to be "becoming the ripple," both personally and professionally. Part one of this book will help you expound on your **Why**, part two explores the significance of your **Action**, part 3 equips you with tools to explore your **Voice,** part 4 is all about the implications of your relationship with your work **Environment**, and part 5–quite possibly my favorite part–is about clarifying your **Special Touch.** I'm excited about what you'll gain through this book, which has insights that have literally impacted the lives of professionals around the world.

I'll be sharing several client stories throughout this book to illustrate certain concepts in action. I've received permission from each client to share their story and have changed names, locations, and various details to preserve their anonymity.

The correlation between your "why" and your financial outcomes

Though there are so many reasons why people push past their challenges in such awe-inspiring ways, the common denominator is a sometimes unrealistic will to do what they are truly meant to do and to be what they are truly meant to be. This push for greatness often comes from their "why."

Amber was a senior-level professional in the technology sector who dreamed of retiring in her 40s. She ultimately wanted to retire young to live her dream life–traveling around the world, hiking in beautiful places, and having multiple rental properties to continue building wealth even after retirement. Her one caveat for retiring early was that she wanted to have substantial capital at the time of her retirement to feel like she was financially comfortable enough to fund her dream life.

Amber attained a 105% salary increase and promotion, allowing her to move multiple levels higher into a much more senior role within her tech company. This promotion came after we worked on creating an actionable plan for her to attain that promotion. We delved into several concepts that I'll be covering in future chapters and other concepts that I'm often supporting 1:1 and corporate teams with, including building a village of advisors through additional mentors and sponsors at work, enhancing her reputation and influence among colleagues across the company, taking her approach to presenting at work to the next level, and finding opportunities for her to participate in initiatives at work where her skills and talents could shine.

Amber's "why" was being able to live her dream life ten years from when we started working together. It was her vision of traveling the world, hiking up mountains, experiencing the bliss of trip after trip, and having a substantial disposable income to spend on her heart's desire. This vision she put in front of her drove her approach to her work daily. It allowed her to push through challenging times at work. It allowed her to understand the importance of creating key connections at work. It also helped her to pursue a higher role at work that she may not have otherwise.

Your "why" for you is whatever you feel drives you to do more than you might naturally desire to do personally or professionally. It is what you may have thought of if you ever lacked motivation to continue working through a task or if you ever considered halting your efforts to do a challenging or uncomfortable task or role and decided to keep going. Maybe your "why" allowed you to complete your college degree, prevented you from quitting a job, or caused you to take on a higher-level role at work with more responsibility, even if it meant being out of your comfort zone.

Examples of what your "why" could be

Here are a few examples of what your "why" could be regarding the work you do professionally. Explore what your top 3 might be:

- **Community:** You love the feeling of community you get at work, and doing great work makes you feel like you're contributing significantly to your colleagues.

- **Financial Freedom:** The desire to have wealth and disposable income to spend on whatever you would like.

- **Honoring a Loved One:** You do the work you do and maybe even do it in a certain way in honor of a mentor, family member, or someone else who had a significant impact on you. That person directly or indirectly inspired you to do great work for several reasons. They may have also helped you expand your vision of the success you could have through your work.

- **Legacy Building:** You want your children and your children's children to have the financial success, degrees, or experiences you have had.

- **Mentorship:** Your desire to operate with excellence or get promoted comes from you wanting to be an example for other colleagues you want to serve as an example for.

- **Peace:** You feel like success brings you more peace through the experiences, living situation, or financial success you have, so you put forth quite a bit of effort in what you do in order to have more of that peace.

- **Spirituality:** You are driven intensely by the spiritual or religious practices you follow that cause you to put forth great effort in what you do and how you do it.

- **Time Freedom:** You know that a certain kind of income or a certain kind of work in a specific role gives you the flexibility to do what you'd like when you'd like to do it, whether that means spending more time with family or having more time to relax.

Knowing your "why" is absolutely key to moving forward, even when challenges come your way. You may not be striving for the 105% income increase and promotion that Amber received as a result of clearly identifying her "why." However, maybe clarifying your "why" would allow you to have more peace, flexibility, freedom, or something else that would be a game changer for you and your life.

Not knowing your "why" can hinder you from going as far as you know you can go. Have you ever participated in an activity growing up and either you only participated for a few days or weeks or you really disliked your experience there? Most likely, it's because you didn't have a strong enough "why" for participating or maybe you didn't have a "why" at all that was aligned with what you were doing. You didn't have a North Star that would anchor you or pull you to continue and not quit. I have clients who have shifted directions with certain goals because they realized their original role did not resonate with them.

And like Amber, knowing your "why" can push you further faster. It can quite literally cut in half the amount of time it takes you to reach whatever pinnacle of success it is that you're striving for. It can allow you to become what you have the potential to be, and the sky's the limit for whatever that is.

What you can do right now

Getting clarity on our why is so important. Here are a few action steps you can take to seek further clarity on your greatest motivations:

- **Reflect.** Sometime this week, take time to reflect on your top motivations for pursuing the professional success you desire, for whatever success looks like for you at work. Be sure to include no more than 3 to really hone in on what's most important to you. These 1- 3 biggest motivations collectively embody your "why." You can jot down what you come up with in a journal, on a blank document, or somewhere you will reference later.

- **Write.** Write about why these top areas of motivation are important to you.

- **Make reflecting on your why a habit.** Consider adding to your calendar weekly, monthly, or quarterly a reminder to refer back to what you reflected on as your biggest "why" for your approach to what you do. I actually have an event in my calendar every morning to reflect on my "why."

As you're continuously becoming the ripple, know that your commitment to getting clearer on your why and being intentional about that has an exponential impact on those around you. I hope that reflecting on this regularly is as meaningful for you as it has been for me. And my hope is also that you also see what practically can happen for you and your work when you get clearer on your "why."

CHAPTER 2

Put Your Why in Front of You

"Keep your eyes on the stars and your feet on the ground."
– Theodore Roosevelt

It can be great to know what truly drives us through knowing our "why," but because our lives are most often so busy, it can be hard to actually remember what is driving us and why that is so important to us. Suppose you think about a competitive track star, for example. In that case, for that athlete to run his fastest race and to avoid slowing down or stopping altogether, the athlete must have a goal in mind and a reason to substantiate why it's so important to continue moving forward at an optimal speed. That's true of our lives, too. Think about what you do daily. There quite literally has to be a significant reason for us to do many of the major things that we do. There's a reason why you work regularly, why you greet people the way you do, or why you communicate with certain family members regularly. But when was the last time you stopped and reflected on why you are so motivated to do what you do? Maybe you already reflect on this regularly but for many individuals, not having your why in front of you enough can hinder you from running your professional race at optimal speed. It can be the difference between being a good team member or being the individual who gets chosen for the opportunity of a lifetime at work. It can be the difference between being a manager people respect versus a manager whose team produces some of the highest results within a company. Or, as a chief executive officer, knowing your why can be the difference between bringing in a respectable annual revenue or doubling your revenue within your company.

Changing your focus can drastically impact your professional outcomes

In Bethany's case, she was the founder and chief executive officer of an award-winning interior design company. She sought out my firm's support amid her company experiencing major revenue issues consistently for almost a year after previously experiencing over ten years of success. She didn't know what had shifted and thought my firm might be able to help. Unfortunately, she was on the verge of filing bankruptcy when she first sought my firm's support.

I can remember feeling the sadness in her voice when we first chatted about her situation. Fortunately, within the 3-month mark of our work together, Bethany's monthly revenue had tripled, which means that her take-home pay drastically increased due to her significant revenue increase. What happened, you might be wondering? Among other things, we realized that Bethany needed to go back to what motivated her to be successful and to engage with that regularly in practical ways. **Here were some of Bethany's top motivations:**

- **Money:** Bethany dreamed of buying a luxury car and renovating her kitchen.

- **Service:** Bethany desired to someday launch a nonprofit for youth with significant financial needs.

- **Mindset:** Bethany and I realized that she had struggled with feeling she wasn't good enough as a businesswoman and leader, and being able to shift this way of thinking into enhancing her self-confidence was a huge motivation for Bethany.

Bethany did several things to triple her revenue. For starters, she put her why in front of her as she tried to revitalize her business. Here are a few ways she put her why in front of her, leading to her company tripling its revenue.

- **Visualization:** Bethany began to visualize her luxury car and renovated kitchen daily to increase her mind's chances of thinking that this dream could come to fruition. **Why this works:** According to an article in Psychology Today, brain studies show that mental imagery influences several brain processes including memory, perception, and planning. As a result, the brain can be trained to help you more confidently perform specific actions or tasks through visualization.[1] Consider Olympic athletes who often do visualization exercises to enhance their performance.

- **Affirmations:** When Bethany first contacted my firm, she didn't fully believe that her company could flourish. Bethany started to incorporate statements throughout the day about who she was and what she could have as (as if she already had it) when it came to what she desired to have and what she desired to do as a result of a successful business. She also would state daily affirmations about who she aspired to be. **Why this works:** A medically-reviewed WebMD article shared that positive affirmations can reduce your level of stress, help you to feel a greater sense of wellness, improve performance academically, and help allow you to be more open to behavior change.[2]

- **Podcasts and Videos:** Bethany listened to podcasts and videos aligned with the mindset she aspired to have in her life and business.

---

[1] Snyder, C. R. "Seeing Is Believing: The Power of Visualization." *Psychology Today*, 9 Dec. 2009, www.psychologytoday.com/us/blog/flourish/200912/seeing-is-believing-the-power-visualization.

[2] "Positive Affirmations: What You Need to Know." *WebMD*, WebMD LLC, 27 May 2023, www.webmd.com/balance/what-to-know-positive-affirmations. Accessed 6 Aug. 2024.

She digested content associated with money, business, and mindset, for example, that all worked to shift her mindset and approach to her business. **Why this works:** Based on research about visualization and affirmation, it's quite possible that exposing yourself to individuals, stories, and information associated with where you desire to be can help your mind more greatly believe that what you're listening to is entirely possible. My firm has had other clients in the past who experienced significant shifts in their mindset due in part to regularly listening to podcasts and videos that helped them truly believe they could achieve what they desired.

After implementing the above action steps along with some other key action steps that I'll touch on later in this book, Bethany's business changed with her bringing in 3x the amount of revenue, and her whole demeanor changed as well. Bethany started showing up to our firm's meetings with joy, inspiration, and hope. Bethany's work ethic reflected her new mindset. Bethany's approach to vendors, team members, clients, and her sales process reflected her new mindset. And her business flourished as a result.

Ideas for putting your "why" in front of you regularly

When it comes to what you might want to utilize when putting your why in front of you, there are so many things that you can do and some are tiny shifts that could create a significant impact for you both personally and professionally. Here are a few examples:

- **Visuals (photos, images, objects):** You could place one or more photos, images (including written messages), or objects around your work area that help inspire you to move towards success. Examples of this are having a vision board around your work area, a photo of your family, or a rock your beloved family member gave you that inspires you to keep pushing. This could be a phrase or longer statement you've written on your bulletin board that motivates you or even your team members as well. For example, one of my firm's clients placed a background on her cell phone that reminded her of her vision and goals in a humorous way.

- **Reading relevant topics:** Whether it's an audiobook, physical book, blog posts, or some other kind of reading, reading can influence the self-talk you might be experiencing at work and allow you to be more aligned with the thoughts you would like to think about success, taking on more complex work, engaging successfully with direct reports, managing up, and more.

- **Progress charts:** Create a visual that tracks your priorities, project targets, milestones, or strategic plan implementation progress regularly within your line of sight at work. As you progress, this tool can allow you to experience positive reinforcement towards the goals you have that matter most.

- **Quotes or affirmations:** Quotes and affirmations, including excerpts from books that have inspired you or equipped you well, when placed around your workspace, can give you the jolt you need when you feel your work has become routine, when challenges come your way, or when new opportunities arise that you might not yet know how to navigate.

- **Achievement reminders:** Diplomas, certificates, trophies, awards, and other symbols of your achievement can remind you to continue to move forward based on your past successes and your capability to tap into more of your potential.

For a list of examples of what you might place around you to increase your motivation, please go to www.becomingtheripple.com.

Whether you desire to triple your company's revenue like Bethany, or you want to be the best you can be for your customers or you're trying to reach your next level professionally when it comes to your position at work, placing your why in front of you can be one of the actions you take that could have a significant impact on your professional trajectory.

What you can do right now

There are so many ways to put your why in front of you daily to accelerate your impact. Here is some guidance about what you can do to make your why have a more prominent presence in your personal and professional life.

- **Identify items that reflect your why.** Consider identifying 1, 2, or 3 items that you can have in your professional space to remind you of your why.

- **Schedule in adding your why to your space.** Schedule when you might add those items to your space.

- **Schedule periodic reflection.** Daily, monthly, or quarterly, schedule taking a few seconds or even a few minutes to really look at whatever you have around you that embodies your why. Reflect on why these items or phrases are so significant in this season. Reflect on what it looks like to operate fully with your why in mind. What would you do differently? How would you be?

If you are to be in a process of continuous growth for yourself and continuous impact on others, becoming the ripple, then continuously putting your why in front of you will be key in this process. This regularly occurring reflection can help prevent you from feeling stuck in a routine that is not serving you or your goals best.

CHAPTER 3
Stay Ready

"The pessimist sees difficulty in every opportunity. The optimist sees opportunity in every difficulty." – Winston Churchill

One young man I mentored in his personal and professional development once asked me, "Out of all of the advice that you would give to anyone, what is the *most* important piece of advice you would give?" After pausing to think about the best answer to that question, my response to him was, "Have your armor ready." I went on to explain what that meant. "Life will bring its challenges your way. We don't know what those challenges might look like, personally, professionally, or otherwise. But what we can do is have an armor of perseverance, resilience, peace, hope, or whatever it is you need, to be ready to fight those battles."

My advice to my mentee was essentially always to be ready–to stay ready–when it comes to preparing for your challenges. Using the "why" you explored earlier in this book can help you identify your reasons for moving forward in doing what you're meant to do even when challenges come your way. Staying ready is also about always making sure you're as prepared as possible for both challenges and opportunities when it comes to your mindset and daily approach to your life both personally and professionally.

Using our habits to "stay ready"

Preparing for challenges and opportunities can happen through understanding the power of our daily habits that contribute to our success. According to the research of Charles Jennings, director of neurotechnology at the MIT McGovern Institute for Brain Research, we have specialized connections in our brain that send up to 1,000 signals per second that ultimately produce one thought.[3] This means we have about one thought per second and around 60,000 thoughts per day on average. These thoughts come as a result of external stimuli that trigger each thought. External stimuli include what we see, hear, touch, taste, or smell–they relate to our sensory receptors. For example, picking up a book, getting into your car, feeling your blanket touch your bare feet, or even hearing the voice of a family member all trigger a specific thought through a series of signals in your brain. In the same way, at work, hearing the voice of your supervisor, sitting down at your desk, or seeing a specific colleague, can all trigger a particular thought.

A study published by the Journal of Personality and Social Psychology also shared that 40 - 45 percent of what we do daily is habitual.[4] That means that 40 - 45 percent of what we do happens automatically every day–that's almost half of what we do every day. Our habits are usually in response to:

- External cues like location or events: For example, I found that when I work on my laptop from the kitchen, I tend to snack maybe twice as much as when I do work on my laptop from my office space located away from the kitchen.

---

[3] https://engineering.mit.edu/engage/ask-an-engineer/what-are-thoughts-made-of/

[4] Wood, W., Quinn, J. M., & Kashy, D. A. (2002). Habits in everyday life: Thought, emotion, and action. *Journal of Personality and Social Psychology, 83*(6), 1281–1297. https://doi.org/10.1037/0022-3514.83.6.1281

- Internal cues: Feeling stressed, for example, might cause certain people to tap their pencils on a table, sigh, procrastinate, or bite their nails.

- Rewards: Our brains release dopamine, a neurotransmitter associated with pleasure when we take a habitual action. This dopamine serves as positive reinforcement for us to continue to implement a specific habit.[5]

For example, let's imagine that Abigail truly desires to pursue a project management certification that can result in a $30,000 increase in pay and a promotion to a new role at work that she would be much more interested in. Still, whenever she desires to study in the evenings after work, she finds that she goes on social media instead. In this case here is what happens to Abigail:

1. **Right after eating dinner and then turning on the dishwasher:**
   a. An external cue, namely Abigail turning on the dishwasher, triggers an undesired habit of Abigail sitting down to relax.
   b. Abigail sitting down to relax is an additional external cue that triggers her negative habit of then watching videos on YouTube and perusing social media posts on the couch.

Unbeknownst to her, Abigail's brain might release dopamine due to her engaging in this habit, causing her to do it repeatedly. In this case, months after deciding to spend time studying for her project management certification exam, Abigail may be frustrated at her lack of desired progress.

One of our challenges as humans is that our natural response to specific triggers is not operating to our benefit. Maybe you can connect with Abigail's desire to do one thing while feeling a pull to do another. However, there is

---

[5] Schultz, W., Dayan, P., & Montague, P. R. (1997). A neural substrate of prediction and reward. *Science*, 275(5306), 1593-1599. doi:10.1126/science.275.5306.1593

hope. You can train yourself to respond differently to external or internal cues by attaching a reward to a specific new habit that replaces an old habit. For example, in Abigail's case, maybe instead of grabbing her phone and sitting on the couch after turning on the dishwasher, let's say that instead, she attempts to form a new habit.

1. **Right after eating dinner and <u>before</u> turning on the dishwasher:**
   a. Abigail uses the external cue of finishing dinner to trigger her turning on classical music in her home–music that helps her to study.
   b. She then uses the external cue of the classical music turning on to do her "study setup steps."
      i. She places her phone in her purse as the calming classical music is playing.
      ii. Abigail then places her laptop on the table.

2. **After turning on the dishwasher:**
   a. Abigail uses turning on the dishwasher as an external cue to trigger a new positive habit. After turning on the dishwasher, she sets a 30-minute countdown timer with an alarm.
   b. Abigail starts to study after turning on the dishwasher and setting her countdown timer.
   c. When the 30-minute countdown timer alarm goes off, Abigail uses that as an external cue that triggers another positive habit. She takes a study break where she gets to make her favorite tea–lemon ginger tea.
   d. Abigail uses this lemon ginger tea as a reward and as positive reinforcement for her new positive habit. She takes her lemon ginger tea back to the dinner table.
   e. Before she starts drinking her lemon ginger tea at the dinner table, she sets a 1-hour countdown timer, reminding herself to set

   countdown timers for each study session to help her focus for short bursts of time.
 f. She then gets to drink her lemon ginger tea as she finishes the next hour of her study session. Her 1-hour countdown timer would mark the end of her study session.

In this example, Abigail successfully creates a new series of positive habits in response to her trigger of finishing dinner. She played classical music and did her study setup steps before turning on the dishwasher. She sets countdown timers to allow her to study in short bursts of time that work best for her to focus. Collectively, these habits will enable her to study successfully for her project management certification exam. This transformation of her evening habits can change Abigail's life. She can be happier at work. She can feel more accomplished when it comes to her goals. The right habits can change *your* life.

Breaking your negative habits

Are you aware of the negative habits you must break to get to where you'd like to be personally or professionally? Based on our average of around 60,000 thoughts per day, we most likely all have habits we are unaware of that are not aligned with who we aspire to be. The idea of staying ready when it comes to these habits is using our greatest motivations, which we identified in Chapter 1, to provide us with a greater desire to shift our negative habits into more positive ones to change our personal and professional outcomes.

It can seem overwhelming to identify what negative habits need to be shifted if we have so many thoughts daily, but it's possible. Have you heard the phrase, "How do you eat an elephant? One bite at a time." One of the things you can challenge yourself to do is to choose just one habit to work on changing at a time. Maybe you work on one new habit that is of the greatest priority for you to change every month, focusing every day of the month on shifting how you approach a habit that is truly important to you.

Improving one habit at a time

If you work on improving one important habit at a time–let's say you do work on improving one habit per month, that's 12 significant habits changed per year, that's 60 key habits changed every five years, and hundreds of habits you'd be shifting over your lifetime—each of them providing you with the ability to make more of the impact and gain more of the influence that you seek personally and professionally. Know that you don't have to try to change every habit you have that is not a positive habit–that isn't humanly possible and would be overwhelming. You're just working on shifting those habits that mean the most to you based on the most important desires you have for yourself personally and professionally. Be sure to give yourself grace when you are not progressing as much as you'd like. This is where resilience or assessing the importance of this habit comes in.

What you can do right now

Let's delve into how you can try to stay ready when it comes to having habits that connect back to your why and prepare you for both opportunities and challenges.

- **Identify habits to work on.** Think about the first 3 habits you would like to work on for the next 90 days. These habits should allow you to be even more prepared for the success that you seek.

- **Identify when you'll work on those habits.** Identify when you'll start taking action during those 90 days to identify the external or internal cues that trigger each habit. Once you identify the external or internal cues that trigger each habit, you can create new external cues for new positive habits or pair new positive habits with your current external cues.

- **Stay focused on your goal.** It's okay if your first attempts at changing your habits don't pan out how you'd like. Keep shifting and trying new cues and approaches to new positive habits, one at a time, to find what works best for you.

There are certainly challenges that might come up along the way as you are continuously becoming the ripple. Still, with the proper habits in place, you can be more resilient and more prepared to continue moving forward despite those challenges. Remember, you'll approach this path to transform your habits to stay ready just as you would eating an elephant–one bite at a time, steadily moving closer towards the success you seek.

PART II

YOUR ACTION

CHAPTER 4

Explore What Truly Matters

"If we take care of the moments, the years will take care of themselves."
– Maria Edgeworth

Have you ever wanted to ask a manager, mentor, or friend what you could do more to get more of what you desire? What if I told you (or reminded you) that the proper answer to this isn't what you think? What if the answer to accomplishing more was based *less on the quantity* of what you're doing but *more on the quality* of what you strategically are doing with your time?

In 2014, I was honored as a finalist for the Washington, D.C. Capital Cause Changemaker of the Year Award. At that time in my life, even though on the outside, it seemed as if I was thriving professionally and personally, I was falling asleep while driving to and from community or networking events, even taking naps in my car in the parking lot of local McDonalds or other businesses between leaving work and heading to an event or meeting. I was also receiving accolades at work in my public affairs role, launching some successful campaigns, getting us featured in major news media, and being honored for maximizing the use of our CRM at work, among other things. At that same time in my life, I would take naps in my car in a secluded space in our work parking lot during lunchtime due to my lack of work-life balance. I was genuinely struggling to manage the various pieces of my life, and I knew that, even with the accolades I received, this impacted my ability to be most effective in any area. Something had to change.

Believe it or not, what we do outside of work to manage our time, self-care, and energy are as important as what we do during work. Each aspect of our life impacts the other. Have you ever noticed that you have peers who come into work more energized, more ready to confidently take on challenges, more reflective when faced with difficult decisions, or even more calm and strategic amid difficult conversations? That clarity, confidence, and calm might come partially from what that peer prioritizes outside of work.

Creating your ideal weekly plan

After realizing something needed to change with my daily routine, one day, I had the idea to create what I deemed as "The Perfect Plan" for what I wanted my days and weeks to look like ideally. I found a basic daily agenda spreadsheet that broke the time in a day into 30-minute increments. I typed into the worksheet what I would do if each hour of my day outside of work was spent doing what I truly desired. I realized I needed to make time for rest after work. I wanted to spend more time talking with my boyfriend (who is now my husband) in the evenings. I wanted to reach out to mentees, friends, and colleagues who I cared about from the past. After I created my ideal daily plan, it suddenly became much more apparent what I might want my ideal week to look like. I opened my Google Calendar and created time blocks associated with what I wanted to do and during what timeframes. I wanted my calendar to align with what I truly prioritized. From Sunday through Saturday, I finally felt like I had a vision for what my life could look like that would provide me with more of a sense of peace, calm, and even fulfillment.

I took a few moments to take a good, hard look at the ideal schedule that I created, and it blew me away. It helped me to identify what I truly prioritized. And what I truly prioritized in some way surprised me. I wondered why I wasn't already doing these things more and realized it was because I simply hadn't stopped and truly reflected on what I wanted. We all have times in our lives when, in one aspect of our lives, professionally or personally, we haven't yet taken a good, hard look to double-check if what we are doing in any area of our lives is what we genuinely desire to prioritize.

After creating my ideal weekly plan, I decided to do the intentional work of having some critical conversations to close out my participation in some initiatives and organizations that I was a part of or about to be a part of. I realized I needed to make more time for what I now knew I desired most. I utilized my weekly plan as a guide to take specific action steps to achieve my vision.

Here is a sample of one day of a completed daily plan spreadsheet in 30-minute increments:

	Monday
5:30 a.m.	Meditation/ Prayer
6:00 a.m.	Journaling
6:30 a.m.	Exercise at Gym
7:00 a.m.	↓
7:30 a.m.	Breakfast
8:00 a.m.	Get ready for work
8:30 a.m.	Work from home
9:00 a.m.	↓
10:00 a.m.	↓
10:30 a.m.	Quick walking break
11:00 a.m.	Working
11:30 a.m.	↓
12:00 p.m.	Lunch break
12:30 p.m.	Working
1:00 p.m.	↓
1:30 p.m.	↓
2:00 p.m.	↓
2:30 p.m.	Quick meditation
3:00 p.m.	Working
3:30 p.m.	↓
4:00 p.m.	↓
4:30 p.m.	↓
5:00 p.m.	Wrap up work
5:30 p.m.	Take a walk/ Call friend
6:00 p.m.	Prepare dinner
6:30 p.m.	Eat dinner
7:00 p.m.	TV/ Leisure time
7:30 p.m.	↓
8:00 p.m.	Call family
8:30 p.m.	Prepare for bed
9:00 p.m.	Journal/ Plan next day
9:30 p.m.	Reading time
10:00 p.m.	Bed time
10:30 p.m.	↓

Here is a sample of a completed weekly plan from an online calendar with time blocks:

For a blank copy of a daily plan spreadsheet and weekly plan, please go to www.becomingtheripple.com.

Your actions within and outside of work can show if your why is truly aligned with how you're showing up in these spaces. In my case, it took for my life outside of work to feel so overwhelming that I was *forced* to pause and take a good, hard look at how I prioritized my time outside of work. If my why at that time was associated with a heart for service, for example, then falling asleep on the road to and from events regularly is not actually aligned with that why. Do you take the time to stop and reflect on what's most vital for you to focus on outside of work based on what is truly important to you? I've realized that we should assess at least every quarter if our daily or weekly routine aligns with our why or if we need to adjust these routines based on what's most important to us in this season. For example, making time for more rest, exercise, meditation, writing, attending a family member's events, or even traveling might be more important in one season of your life versus the other.

Regularly taking the wrong actions professionally can regularly take you down the wrong path

My family loves banana bread. And there have been times when we didn't have the baking powder we needed to make the banana bread. In those instances, we just use baking soda without baking powder–don't judge me! Though the banana bread still tastes great to my family, the baking powder impacts the physical appearance of the banana bread because the baking powder actually helps the banana bread to rise, so the banana bread will have a denser texture without it. Using baking soda without baking powder also makes the banana bread taste more bitter. The reason why is that baking soda is a base that requires acid to activate it, and the baking powder has both an acid and a base that allows for the banana bread to rise nicely.

Have you ever felt like the mix of the activities you were doing in your professional life wasn't producing the outcome you wanted? It could be that adding more of the right ingredients and maybe less of the misaligned ingredients to your daily schedule could completely change your outcomes.

A salesperson who isn't making sales as they should may have decreased revenue or commissions over time. An online marketing professional who spends too much time on design and not enough time on how followers are engaging with content may not have as much success with their marketing efforts. A founder and business owner spending too much time on unimportant logistics and not enough time focusing on the most critical sales, marketing, and customer experience efforts, could experience much slower growth than they would like.

One of the things that stops people from going further faster is that they are taking the wrong action. Like my story of creating my ideal plan, how would someone know if their action isn't producing the right outcomes if they haven't stopped and thought about what the right mix of daily activity might look like? They might not. Regularly reflect on what your ideal life could look like from day-to-day and week-to-week to rise to the level you desire, both personally and professionally.

What you can do right now

You can certainly take more actions within and outside of work that align with your why. Here are a few steps that you might try.

- **Set aside time.** Carve out 1 hour over the next 30 days for you to create your ideal daily and weekly plan. You may only look at your current calendar once you create your first draft to explore unlimited possibilities.

- **Create the plan.** Create "The Perfect Plan" for what your ideal day and week looks like, considering what is practically important for you to integrate into your plan and what you could realistically do or not do that would provide you with more of what you desire in life.

- **Adjust.** After creating the plan, schedule about 1 hour for you to take action to adjust your calendar using your usual calendar tool(s). Reach out to individuals you might need to have a critical conversation with about some things that need to change on your calendar and take any other necessary actions to ensure you can implement "The Perfect Plan" for what you would like to prioritize.

Some people think that others who are successful are simply made that way when, often, those individuals have some way of consistently working towards whatever they desire. For them to be continuously becoming the ripple, it usually goes back to how they intentionally spend their time regularly. Think of your favorite athlete, or your most coveted mentor, or your favorite supervisor, or your favorite performer. They all likely commit to consistently being intentional with key components of their time. Regularly assess your daily and weekly routines to ensure they are contributing to the personal and professional success you desire.

CHAPTER 5

Practice Targeted Time

"He who is everywhere is nowhere."
– Seneca

When I was in college, I volunteered as a summer camp counselor at a camp for kids with terminal illnesses during a few summers. The camp was called Camp Boggy Creek and was based out of a beautiful, wooded area with lovely ponds and lakes in Eustis, FL. My first summer at the camp was the first time I experienced a campfire, archery, and canoeing as someone who grew up in North Miami Beach, FL. When it came to archery, it was essential to have a high-quality arrow and a high-quality target for the person doing the archery (let's call them the archer) to be able to hit their target effectively. The archer's goal is to hit the highest-scoring zone of the target right in the center of the target, called the bullseye.

How we manage our time in our professional endeavors should be like how we would ensure we hit a bullseye most efficiently with an arrow. Our actions should be like our arrows. We must ensure that we place the right action steps on our calendar by identifying the most significant priorities for our professional work. Placing the wrong priorities on our calendars is a sure way for us to feel distracted, discouraged, and disappointed. Placing the right priorities on our calendars makes us feel more focused, encouraged, and satisfied. After all, we only have 24 hours in a day.

The bullseye on the target-that highest scoring zone-should represent the timeframe we work most effectively during our day. We can call this our "primary focus" time, just as this would be your primary focus in archery. Your primary focus time is when you are most alert, feel like you can conquer the day, and have the best chance of most effectively accomplishing your goals. It's important to know what this timeframe is on your calendar because if you place the action steps that would make the most significant impact on your role, department, or business (your arrow) on the timeframe on your calendar when you have the highest chances of knocking a task out of the ballpark (your bullseye), great things would happen. Imagine that as a result of doing this consistently for 30 days, moving the needle incrementally every day on your most critical goals by even 10%, you would accomplish several vital goals over time.

For me, that primary focus time is between 6:30 a.m. - 9:30 a.m. every morning. One of the most significant ways I completed this book was to write every morning during that very time frame. I created marketing pieces when working in public affairs or as an editor for different publications by doing my most complex writing during the morning timeframe.

And of course, there are other areas outside of the very center of the target-outside of the bullseye-that are still great for your arrow to hit when you're doing archery. Let's consider those times that are not the very best timeframes as "secondary focus" timeframe targets. You can keep in mind that you are alert and ready to do complex work even at those time frames and place important and complex work that might not be primary priorities during that time. For example, suppose a secondary focus timeframe target for me might be 9:30 a.m. - 12 p.m.. In that case, I know maybe that would be a great time to complete strategic planning work, strategy meetings where complex ideas are important to propose, having sales conversations with prospective clients, or preparing key marketing pieces that require a high level of creativity for example.

The outside layer of the target could exemplify when your mind feels least productive but where you still need to be productive. We'll call this timeframe your "tertiary focus" time. For many people, that might be at the end of their work day. Maybe the arrows that are pointed at that part of your target focus on important activities that do not require a complex level of strategic thought or are not as important but do need to be accomplished.

Here's a visual illustration of what targeted time looks like:

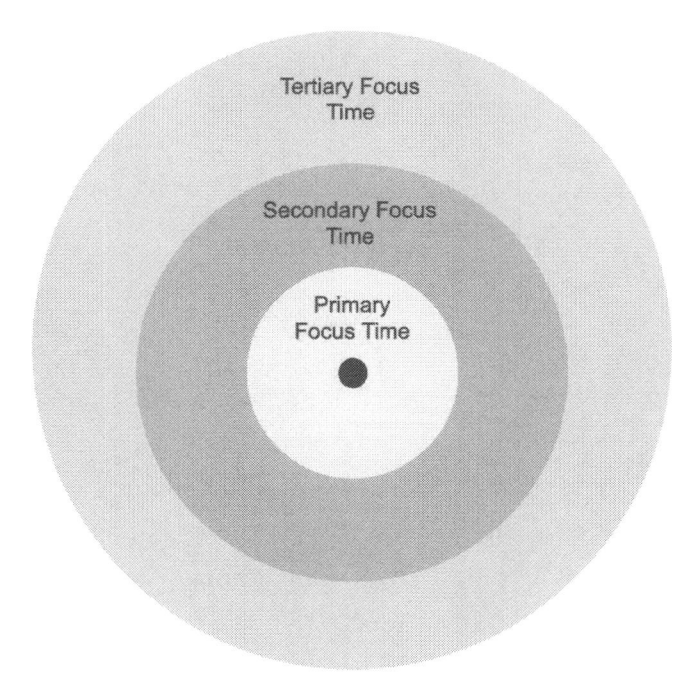

Tertiary Focus Time

Secondary Focus Time

Primary Focus Time

One of my leadership development clients, Bridgett, led marketing efforts for a school district in a very senior role that was one of the highest-level positions within a school district. She had many priorities and individuals reporting to her or leaning on her for guidance and action. Bridgett needed a way to feel more organized, as she had many competing priorities in her role. She also needed a way to continue to address her role's strategic priorities regularly. One of the things our firm supported Bridgett with for her to manage her priorities further while keeping her strategic plan priorities at the forefront was helping her to create an end-of-day close-out routine. This routine occurred during the last hour of Bridgett's work day, during her tertiary focus time.

Within her close-out routine, she incorporated soft music, a reflection on wins for the day along with prospective shifts to be made for her approach to the next day, answering essential emails, identifying any action steps that needed to be accomplished as a result of the activities and meetings of the current day, and assessing what needed to be prioritized for the next day and for the remainder of the week. Bridgett's approach to her end-of-day close-out routine is an example of strategically utilizing your tertiary focus time, where you still have goals to complete at work but want to be strategic about what arrows are hitting which part of your target.

Where do emails fit in Targeted Time?

Sometimes, we have action items that are not at all a primary or secondary focus but need to be placed within higher priority timeframes because they just can't wait to be done during less optimal time frames in our day. An example of that is checking email. In 2024, emails and how to manage them have become increasingly more challenging for many people, as marketers, colleagues, key stakeholders professionally, friends, and organizations are all sending emails daily. It is worth sharing about this here because email management often comes up as a topic that impacts productivity, based on feedback from several of our firm's clients.

Though email can be overwhelming, managing it often can't be ignored. An email that seems insignificant may actually be important from the sender's perspective. Or maybe being responsive quickly to emails or messages through an online platform is extremely important within your organization's culture. Scheduling multiple blocks of time per day for administrative tasks like email within your primary or secondary focus time can be essential to maintain or enhance your reputation in the workplace.

In Bridgett's case, she scheduled three one-hour time blocks for checking email in the morning, early afternoon, and late afternoon while she was at work. These different timeframes for checking email allowed her to work towards an empty inbox by the end of her business day, not be overwhelmed with answering emails at the end of the day, and not miss out on any important emails that may have come through that deserved her immediate attention. During Bridgett's designated time blocks for checking email, some emails were placed in folders and marked as unread, some were responded to, some were deleted, and some were kept in her primary inbox and marked as unread.

Utilizing targeted time for your daily work routine

A top-notch daily routine could be created from understanding the right activities–or arrows–to place on your primary focus timeframes–your bullseye, the right activities to place on your secondary focus timeframes–the other high-scoring zones on your target, and the right activities to place on your tertiary focus timeframes–the most outlying area on your target.

For example, based on this strategy, you could decide where to place your stakeholder engagement email outreach, strategic planning time, data analysis, and direct report check-ins.

What to do if targeted time is not working for you

If you try this method of targeted time over a period of time–for a week for example–and see that it's not working for you, identify what might need to shift in your work routine, and adjust until you have a system that works for you. For example, you may find that based on your meeting schedule at work, your primary focus time in one time block is not enough time for you to get your priorities done throughout the day. Or you might find that you never get to your tertiary focus time. Keep shifting and experimenting with new ways of implementing your work routine, and know that time management is often a work in progress as you look to find what's most sustainable for you.

You might find that, based on your job role, urgent action items that might fit into your primary or secondary focus categories come up throughout the day. If that is the case, after assessing if the activity is truly a priority, you might decide to take care of primary focus time activities first even during tertiary focus timeframes in order to meet or exceed the expectations of your team or customers, transitioning right back into whatever your established routine is after completing the priority.

Also, utilize the idea of the compound effect to help targeted time work for you. Think of taking small steps to utilize targeted time little by little. For example, you might find that you might focus on mastering your primary focus time first and will start with the small step of blocking your calendar from 8 a.m. - 10 a.m. every morning as a senior leader so that no meetings are scheduled during that time if that works well for your workplace. You might strictly adhere to having no morning meetings during that time even if you're tempted to schedule them there, knowing that your business development outreach activities, your most important priority, will exponentially increase if you stick to this. This commitment might result in a promotion for you, exponentially more revenue coming into your company, an improved reputation among your peers, manager, and direct reports, and a greater sense of overall peace for you within and outside of work.

What you can do right now

If you're placing the right activities in the right time frames and can tackle your priorities with clarity and focus, that can be a game-changer for you. Here are a few steps you can take to implement this.

- **Identify your timeframes.** Identify what time frames during your work day would be best for primary focus time, secondary focus time, and tertiary focus time. Consider what time frames would be best based on team meetings or other components of your work schedule that are not currently within your realm of control, being clear on what timeframes are definitely within your control to shift. Establish also what timeframes might need to be placed on your daily work schedule for administrative work if needed.

- **Identify your priorities.** Identify what major ongoing activities should be placed within each time frame. For a blank copy of a targeted time planning document, please go to www.becomingtheripple.com.

- **Add to your scheduling tool.** After you've created your plan for utilizing targeted time, add your schedule to your favorite calendar or planning tool to utilize your plan within your work. Adjust your plan as needed, assessing what works best for you to implement based on the context of your work, your team, your work culture, and your intentions.

The process of becoming the ripple consistently as a professional and creating a sustained ripple effect on your work and others requires an intentional approach to identifying and implementing priorities. Remember, what is applied at work can often also be applied personally. You can conduct this same activity for yourself in regard to your time outside of work. The exercise of figuring out our arrows and targets in our personal lives is also a great exploration of what our lives look like. Is there a great emphasis on your health, family, self-care, or spiritual growth, for example? You can see where you'd like to shift pretty quickly after doing this exercise for your out-of-work time, especially when it comes to your primary focus timeframe. And just as you would do for your work planning, shift your personal schedule as needed, assessing what works best for you to live more of the kind of life that you desire.

CHAPTER 6

Use the Rule of 3s

"Do what you can, with what you have, where you are."
– Theodore Roosevelt

I once heard an interview with an international productivity and performance expert about why smart people underperform. This expert, Dr. Edward Hallowell, M.D., is also a board-certified psychiatrist and serves as a world-renowned authority on ADHD. He had worked on productivity and performance with athletes, corporate business leaders, and others internationally. He realized that one of the reasons why people underperform is that they set way too many goals and end up accomplishing none of them (or very little of them). I believe this concept can apply to businesses that have way too many goals; professionals who set way too many goals for what to accomplish in a day, week, or month; families that have way too many goals; and of course also for individuals who have too many goals.

Too many good intentions can result in a lack of action

On my 27th birthday, I traveled to Florida for a good friend's wedding. I decided to spend time on my birthday reflecting on my goals while at a beach, with its calming water, beautiful sand, and radiant sun. It was the perfect scene. I felt the wind blowing gently around me as I wrote about 20 goals I wanted to accomplish in a notebook. However, I literally never opened that notebook up again to check out those goals. *And I have no earthly idea to this day where that notebook is.*

There were a few issues with this scenario. I had no sustainable plan for implementing the goals I wrote. When would I go back to review these goals? Where would I ensure they were written so they would be in front of me regularly? When would I spend time to implement these goals? Also, I had way too many goals–an issue that the international productivity and performance expert I referenced earlier cited as being problematic.

Dr. Hallowell shared in his interview that one way to avoid having an excessive number of goals is to hone in on the rule of 3s. He suggested identifying your top three goals for the year, your top three goals for the month, your top three goals for the week, and your top three goals for the day. By honing in on what is of utmost priority for you, you can drastically increase your chances of focusing on accomplishing those goals. This, optimally, is how a strategic plan also works. It should allow everyone in an organization to be laser-focused on achieving the organization's most critical goals, no matter what everyone's individual role is within an organization.

How I used the rule of 3's to hit a $100,000 goal

An example of how this worked in my own firm is that I used to establish many goals for my business that I would rarely reference again throughout the year. Before expanding my team, back when I worked mainly as a solopreneur, the year that my business began to bring in over $100,000 in revenue annually, it was because I used the rule of 3s. Here's how I implemented that practically:

- I focused on having three key goals for the year for each business component including finance, marketing, sales, operations, and professional development.

- I then developed what my top three overall key goals were for that year:
    - Bring in $100,000 in revenue
    - Bring in at least three corporate contracts
    - Attain one new certification

- I scheduled a monthly calendar invite to refer to all of my key goals with a focus on our top three goals. This calendar invite also contained a reminder to schedule any action steps associated with my goals.

I honed in regularly on the action steps I could take to achieve my top three goals that year. For example, to bring in $100,000 that year, I was ensuring that my marketing efforts consistently engaged my specific target market, I ensured that my firm's clients had above-and-beyond customer service resulting in a significant repeat client rate of over 40%, and I took action to seek out new revenue-generating opportunities for my firm. The outcome was that I was able to hit that $100,000 goal.

What you can do right now

I want you to reflect on where you can use the rule of 3s to thrive at work. Where in your professional life, could you have more significant results with greater focus on your priorities? Where do you feel you're not putting the right activities in the right timeframe because you're really not clear on what the right activities are for you to be doing? Where are you not practicing enough targeted time? Here are a few steps you can take to hone in on your top three areas of focus:

- **List your key components.** List the areas of your work that are the key components of what you do.

- **List your priorities.** List the top 5-10 priorities for each work area.

- **Hone in on your top priorities.** Identify the top 3 priorities under each area.

- **Identify your top goals.** Reflect on your complete list and identify the top 3 overall goals that would create the most significant impact that you're looking for in your role. If you work for an organization where your manager's perception of priorities is different than yours, consider what would make the most impact considering your manager's perspectives as well.

The rule of 3's allows you to truly hone in on not only what is good to do, but what is vital to do as you are becoming the ripple. Focusing on your top three priorities and consistently doing so can be the game changer you've been looking for to feel you're creating more impact and being even more successful at work.

PART III

YOUR VOICE

CHAPTER 7

Remember Your 3 Keys

"To be yourself in a world that is constantly trying to make you something else is the greatest accomplishment." – Ralph Waldo Emerson

Even if you know your why and you're taking all of the right actions to pursue professional success, if people are perceiving you negatively, it can completely disrupt your ability to be successful. People's negative perception of you can cause conflict, confusion, frustration, or can even cause you to be belittled or taken advantage of in your work. This is why it's so important to focus as much on how you're perceived in your professional relationships as you focus on the other things we mentioned.

Who do you want to be?

At your core, who do you want to be? To answer this question, it's helpful to think of who you are at your best. Think of how you have been when you have worked best with your colleagues, been most successful in working in groups, or contributed to things going well with you and your managers. You could even ask your friends and family, "How am I when I am at my best?" and learn from them some of what you embody when others perceive you to be at your best. Then, identify three words that most express what it is that you embody when you're at your best. Having three words that synthesize the essence of your best self will make it easier to come back to these words when you need a reminder of who you aspire to be.

This approach also relates to organizations. Organizations should always strive to think about, "At our core, who do we want to be as a company?" Organizations should regularly ask themselves, "Who are we when we are at our best?" The mission or values of an organization can be a great way to see what that organization aspires to in its ideal state.

Cava is a restaurant chain that has experienced significant growth, with its revenue growing 30.3% to $256.3 million in the first quarter of 2024 compared to $196.8 million in the first quarter of 2023.[6] Cava's website states that its mission is "To bring heart, health, and humanity to food." The site expounds on this by stating, "We believe in: Serving delicious food that helps more people eat well and live well. Taking care of the people and things that feed us: the earth, farmers, purveyors, and team members. Food as a unifier, for a more diverse yet inclusive world, where all are welcome."[7] Within the past two years, Cava has become my favorite restaurant chain, especially when I travel. When I see a Cava at an airport or stop by one in a new town, I know that I will get fresh, healthy ingredients and that Cava team members will be respectful and kind. I know the store will have a clean and welcoming feel to it. All of this is aligned with Cava's mission and shows through in how its customers also experience Cava.

In a company setting, every team member in every store and corporate office should be able to communicate the company's mission or values so that it can be embodied daily in practice by every team member and experienced by

---

[6] "CAVA Group Reports First Quarter 2024 Results." *CAVA Group*, 2024, investor.cava.com/news/news-details/2024/CAVA-Group-Reports-First-Quarter-2024-Results/default.aspx#:~=CAVA%20Revenue%20grew%2030.3%25%20to,CAVA%20Restaurants%20year%20over%20year. Accessed 7 Aug. 2024.

[7] "Our Story." *CAVA*, cava.com/ourstory. Accessed 7 Aug. 2024.

every key stakeholder. In the same way, our 3 keys should be so embraced by each of us that we should be able to recall them at any time. Most importantly, we should also strive to embody those 3 keys daily.

Exploring your 3 Keys

For one of the clients who came to my firm for executive coaching support, Clara, she was realizing that her perception of her capabilities wasn't where it should be based on her natural gifts. She had shared that past events in her life had resulted in her having a lower self-perception that impacted her ability to pursue higher positions at work, even as she took on more complicated opportunities regularly. Clara was someone who could flesh out the different key components of challenges and identify what opportunities and perspectives might need to be explored when it came to those challenges. She was a team member who went above and beyond for other team members and was a natural problem solver. When Clara was at her best, she had more confidence. Her head would go up, her shoulders would go back, and her tone would also exude confidence in those moments.

Together, Clara and I came up with a few phrases that described Clara when she was at her best:

- **Self-Generative**
- **Problem Solver, and**
- **Confident.**

What happened after we came up with these phrases was inspiring. Clara focused on the Self-Generative phrase, realizing that no matter what kind of project came up at work and no matter what challenging situation came up in her life when it came to her personal and professional relationships, she could come up with perspectives and opportunities despite the scale of the issue.

For a few weeks, Clara would remind herself of this phrase daily, which changed how she showed up professionally and personally. She realized she was not stuck. She was not experiencing a challenge she couldn't think through. She was not less capable than her colleagues. She remembered that she was self-generative, which impacted her approach to everything she did. This understanding was vital for her to advance professionally and personally. Clara pulled in the problem-solving piece to develop tangible solutions to workplace and personal challenges, working more to exude confidence as a result of utilizing her self-generative and problem-solver characteristics more.

Clara's three words became her "three keys." These three characteristics were foundational to Clara operating as the best version of herself at work. Prior to that, Clara frequently wondered if she could keep up with her work and, at times, felt that she was not as qualified as some of her colleagues. However, after more easily being able to recall her strengths and operating within those strengths more, Clara received accolades for her work in front of her team. She was also provided with an annual bonus following her annual review based on the high quality of the work she produced.

Why identify your 3 keys

Just as Clara used the knowledge of her 3 keys to transform how she showed up at work, you too can utilize this approach to be more aligned with the best version of yourself at work. Identifying who you are at your best can be the foundation for cultivating more work relationships, expanding more significant opportunities at work, and approaching your work with more ease and confidence.

Knowing who you are at your best also allows you to establish a standard for who you aspire to be at work that is not based on comparison. If you are competing with the best version of yourself, then you can more frequently keep imposter syndrome at bay if that might be something you struggle with occasionally. Every day can be a new day to strive for excellence based on what that looks like for you.

The result of knowing your 3 keys isn't only in the tangible benefits at work but also in the peace, joy, and even pride produced when you feel significantly aligned with being your best self.

Knowing your governing principles

Who you aspire to be daily can also be seen as knowing your governing principles or your values. And when you can operate in alignment with those, the results are limitless.

The fantastic manager who everyone wants to work with operates with a specific set of governing principles. Their governing principles might include:

- inspirational leadership,
- always mentoring, and
- innovation.

The phenomenal director of communication who creates award-winning work operates with a set of governing principles. Their governing principles might include:

- be thorough,
- clarity is kind, and
- remembering intention.

Even the loving father who is a beacon of light to his children, operates with a set of governing principles. His might include:

- inspire even when difficult,
- mentoring always, and
- remembering intention.

Did you notice that some of the examples I used in the loving father example also relate to some of the professional examples I used? Operating with your governing principles in mind not only allows you to have greater impact in the workplace but also translates to your impact on your life as a whole.

What you can do right now

Identify your 3 keys so that you can reference them daily or weekly as a consistent visual reminder of who you aspire to be when you're at your best. Here are a few steps you can take to identify your 3 keys:

- **List words or phrases that describe you.** Create a list of 15 words or phrases that embody who you are personally and professionally when you are at your best. Be sure that these words truly resonate with you and your values.

- **Star your top 7.** Write a star next to the top 7 words or phrases that embody who you are personally and professionally when you are at your best.

- **Underline your top 3.** Underline the top 3 words or phrases that embody who you are personally and professionally when you are at your best. These are your 3 keys.

- **Create a visual.** Identify where you will place these 3 words to be able to have them as a visual reminder of who you aspire to be. Some examples of where you can place them are
    - On a sticky note in a prominent location
    - As a pop-up daily or weekly reminder on your phone
    - In a calendar invite that comes up daily or weekly on your phone or computer
    - As a home screen on your phone or computer

You can use this worksheet at www.becomingtheripple.com to identify your three keys.

Everyone has a unique way of becoming the ripple personally or professionally. Consistently focusing on *your* 3 keys can help transform how you show up professionally as you more frequently embody your best self and reap the rewards of what that produces personally and professionally in your life.

CHAPTER 8

Be Who You Aspire to Be

"The journey of a thousand miles begins with one step."
– Laozi

In elementary school, I had a high-pitched voice, blushed a lot, and was never the loudest one in the group. Periodically, I think about how I was such a shy little girl growing up. That greatly contrasts how now, as an adult, as I did just a few days ago, I can be speaking to an audience of hundreds of people, walking through the aisles, and engaging people in content about growing their influence and impact at work. It is surprising how things can so drastically change in every one of us.

To further draw out that point, take a moment and think about one aspect of who you were in your childhood or in your 20s that has since changed. Now, think about what had to happen for that aspect of you to change. In my case, mentors encouraged me to amplify my voice. They wanted me to let others hear my voice more by speaking up and participating in opportunities where I could hone the skills of speaking and leading. Despite what my mentors wanted for me, I had to make a decision to act on my mentors' recommendations based on what they saw in me. Nothing would happen if they saw greatness in me, but I decided not to act.

Even when others in your personal or professional life see greatness in you, if you decide not to act on that perspective, you may not be able to fully embrace your greatness. You have the opportunity daily to be the greatest version of yourself. Even when you know you have the potential to do great things, if you don't act on that potential, you're not able to fully operate in your greatness. However, greatness is in all of us. We must intentionally tap into our greatness, even when it seems far-fetched.

Becoming who you aspire to be to impact a cause

Daria is a nonprofit business owner and founder who came to my firm seeking support in expanding her network to get much-needed resources to grow her nonprofit. Daria shared with me that though she was very accomplished professionally, she had a significant hesitation around networking with others. She wasn't entirely clear about how to approach networking conversations, cultivate relationships, and make strategic asks for resources that could impact the cause that her nonprofit was supporting.

Though my firm was able to provide Daria with support and coaching associated with the tactical pieces of expanding her network, one of the greatest things that needed to happen was that Daria needed to see herself as someone who was a networker. Daria had to feel confident enough to strategically create and cultivate key relationships regularly.

Daria worked on her perception of herself as someone who could masterfully network as she practiced initiating and cultivating networking relationships, and what happened next was truly inspiring. Daria created key contacts throughout her city associated with her nonprofit's cause. She became known for being an advocate and key stakeholder in the topic associated with her nonprofit and gained connections to resources and clients that grew her nonprofit's impact. She moved to another state eventually and was able to again create a strong network of contacts who supported her work to the point where she attained a critical multi-year grant that allowed her to expand services and her impact locally in her new city.

Daria knew who she aspired to be as a networker and knew her why for networking–she wanted to expand her impact on society through her nonprofit organization's work. The more she could be who she aspired to be, the more her work and impact would be expanded.

What to do when you don't feel like being who you aspire to be

Depending on your life circumstances, you may have been raised in a way that you are naturally inclined to ways of being that don't allow you to be your best self. Or perhaps you've met others who seemed naturally inclined not to be their best selves. Maybe you know someone who is naturally inclined to be angry at others as soon as things aren't going their way. Perhaps that's what they saw growing up or from a previous leader. Maybe you've known someone who is easily annoyed with others and it's pushing people away. Perhaps that's how others were with them at some point personally or professionally. Perhaps you know someone who gets nervous about speaking spur of the moment at a meeting. Perhaps that person gets so anxious about speaking spur of the moment because their speaking without having ample time to process what they would say was not met kindly when they had done that in previous aspects of their life. Maybe you know someone who dwells on big decisions for much longer than they'd like in a way that has them being perceived as indecisive. Perhaps you can relate to one of these examples. Whatever it is that you might be naturally inclined towards that doesn't allow you to be your best self, know there are ways to become more of who you aspire to be. Some of the people we have honored most in history have practiced this art of becoming more of who they aspire to be and have become leaders, start-athletes, great orators, and people of great character as a result.

What do you do when you don't feel like being who you aspire to be? What do you do when you don't feel like being known as the strategic thinker, when you don't feel like exuding confidence, when you don't feel like taking the higher ground and remaining professional when someone is disrespectful to you, or when you don't feel like leading your team through tough times? These are all natural feelings, especially when the most challenging circumstances come our way. There are a few things we've covered in earlier chapters that can be helpful to come back to in this instance.

When you don't feel like being who you aspire to be:

- **Go back to your why.** You can reflect, journal, or speak to someone about what motivates you to align most with the values that embody your aspirations.

- **Remember your 3 words.** In the most challenging times, it can be unclear to you who it is that you aspire to be. Your decreased emotional or physical capacity might make you forget who it is that you desire to focus your energy on being. Knowing and retaining knowledge of the 3 words that embody who you aspire to be the most is a quick way to remind yourself of who it is you want to ensure you're being even in challenging times.

- **Establish alignment routines.** Identify what actions you can take daily that will allow you to be in the space to be the best version of yourself when it comes to your 3 words and use targeted time to identify when to do those activities. For example, you might have a daily mindfulness routine that happens right after you wake up, during lunch, and in the evenings. Every morning, you might read at least 1 chapter from a book touching on topics associated with what you aspire to be more of. At the end of your work day, you might have a "Closing routine" that allows you to not only reflect on priorities for the next day and next week, but also enables you to reflect on how you feel you approached the day when it comes to your values, and what you would like to do differently the next day. You may even have routines before, during, or after meetings that help you feel most aligned with your values.

What you can do right now

Do you realize that you're not working towards being more of who you aspire to be on a daily basis? Do you ever feel off of your game, not feeling like you're truly embodying your best characteristics? We all have moments or seasons of life where we feel we're not aligned with being our best selves.

Here are some things you can do right now to be more of who you aspire to be:

- **Write your 3 keys.** Be sure to have your 3 keys, the 3 phrases that embody who you aspire to be, written prominently somewhere you can see them regularly. This can be on a sticky note on a computer, a sticky note on your fridge, or in a daily calendar invite for example.

- **Have an accountability partner.** Find one person you trust who has your best interest in mind to be your accountability partner. This might be a team member, your manager, a colleague who works in another department, or even a family member or friend with whom you might process specific professional challenges or opportunities. Share your 3 keys with this person and ask them to check in with you about how you are doing when it comes to your 3 keys on a weekly or monthly basis or at some other frequency you decide upon. You can ask your accountability partner to observe your actions and approaches to work regularly and share feedback they have that can help you be more aligned with your values.

- **Schedule time to check on your alignment.** Whether you have a mentor, advisor, therapist, accountability partner, or regularly occurring journaling routine, schedule time daily or weekly to identify where you can be more aligned with your values and to determine what you can do to get you closer to where you want to be when it comes to your values.

- **Give yourself grace.** As human beings, we are all imperfect. The goal is to strive for greatness and to know that you either learn or win when it comes to your circumstances. Work to transform your perception of challenges so that they don't seem like losses and instead are clearly lessons. This perspective will allow you to experience the peace needed to thrive amid your circumstances while embodying more of what aligns with your values.

Increasing your success and influence through becoming the ripple is likely not going to be a quick fix, but rather an ongoing project that can be a journey where you learn more and more about yourself as you strive to enhance your growth. Utilizing the tools and strategies above can help you feel supported and at peace as you are on this journey.

CHAPTER 9

Analyze Your Tone

"What you do speaks so loudly that I cannot hear what you say."
– Ralph Waldo Emerson

The Ralph Waldo Emerson quote, "What you do speaks so loudly that I cannot hear what you say" embodies the significance of what you represent through your actions being even more important than what you say. People who have the ability to influence others are not all the same–some are charismatic, or more serious, or generally more reserved, or very humorous, or even more firm. However, every individual who can influence others is able to effectively use their own unique personality and values to influence others effectively.

Think about a colleague who seemed exceptionally equipped to do the tasks associated with their role but was ineffective in coming across respectfully with colleagues, possibly being belittling or aggressive in their approach. I'm secretly hoping that if you're reading this, you've never experienced having this kind of colleague. However, if you have, you most likely observed that their tone impacted their results. Having an ineffective tone that might be too aggressive for your colleagues can result in:

- Confusion because colleagues fear the backlash that comes with asking you questions when they need clarity

- A tarnished reputation

- Colleagues who are highly talented not wanting to work with you

- Colleagues deciding not to give you their total effort based on their diminished loyalty toward you

- Increased turnover as a result of people not feeling psychologically safe

Alternatively, you may have experienced working with a colleague who came across as not as fully confident in themselves. Maybe their tone was largely hesitant. Perhaps, this colleague struggled to ensure their voice was heard at meetings. You may also have observed that their tone impacted their results. Having an ineffective tone when it comes to not being able to share thoughts and perspectives confidently might also have some negative results including:

- Confusion because colleagues are not aware of important details for a project that you may not have felt you had the space to share

- Confusion and teams not working to their full potential because you haven't added innovative ideas or unique perspectives that you have kept to yourself

- A tarnished reputation where colleagues don't feel you can handle more complex work or work where you need to be spotlighted

- Colleagues who are incredibly talented not wanting to work with you

- Colleagues deciding not to give you their total effort based on their diminished loyalty toward you

- Increased turnover as a result of people not feeling confident in your leadership or your role as a team member

- Decreased salary increases or promotions as a result of colleagues not knowing your full potential when it comes to your projects, tasks, contributing, and leading

There are so many approaches to your professional work when it comes to your tone that can either help or hinder you. This is why analyzing your tone is vital to growing your influence and impact.

The most important aspects of communication that influence your impact

When we think of communication, most of us think of vocal communication-the words people say-or written communication-the words we read, where communication is very complex and layered. In my firm's training sessions, when talking about communication, we find it important to emphasize that communication consists of several components including what's going on in the current life and past experiences of the listener, what's happening with the current life and past experiences of the speaker, the tone of the speaker, the body language of the speaker, assumptions of the listener, assumptions of the speaker, distractions, and more.

In fact, according to UCLA behavioral psychologist and professor, Albert Mehrabian, 93 percent of communication happens without words, 55 percent of communication to others is through our body language, and 38 percent is expressed to others through our tone. According to Mehrabian, only 7 percent of our communication happens through our words.[8] According to Mehrabian's research, your body language significantly influences how a message is perceived. This includes your stance, the position of your arms, and your facial expressions. Imagine your manager at a previous job you had

---

[8] Mehrabian, Albert. *Silent Messages: Implicit Communication of Emotions and Attitudes*. Wadsworth Publishing Company, 1981.

sharing with you, "You really did an outstanding job on this project" with a calm, relaxed facial expression or even a smile. You might receive that positively. However, if your manager shared the same message grabbing the sides of his head, shrugging, or furrowing his eyebrows, you would receive the message quite differently. You might question what your manager is saying. You might feel the manager is being dishonest or sarcastic. You might even feel your manager is being quite frustrated with you.

Mehrabian's research also focused on 38 percent of communication happening through your tone. This means that the rising and lowering of your voice–your voice inflection–and the feelings that come through your voice through the speed of your delivery and other factors all matter when it comes to communication. Others can hear joy, hesitation, confidence, aggression, compassion, safety, and more through your voice inflections, therefore they are a significant part of the recipe you need to make an impact. For example, if your team member shares with you, "Yes, I'm clear on your instructions," if that is shared with firmness, and if that is the acceptable culture on your team, that might imply confidence. If that is shared with a tone of confidence, in an upbeat manner, for example, if that is acceptable for the culture of your team, that might imply confidence too. If "Yes, I'm clear on your instructions," is shared with a barely audible voice, in a slow, dragging way, or with increases and decreases in your volume that imply sarcasm, any of those tones might hinder your reputation at work.

Exploring your intentions

Mastering the art of communication only has to be important to you if your why for communicating well matters to you. For example, maybe it matters to you that you keep your job, your team does well, you retain top talent, you don't burn bridges, you are perceived as competent, you're seen as confident, or that you have a good reputation. If any of these things matter to you, then your tone in communication must also matter. The most effective, influential, and impactful communicators understand the importance of knowing their intentions to determine the best way to approach someone else.

For example, if a leader's intention is to be respected by a direct report, then someone with a tone that inflicts fear on team members may not meet that intention. Where respect may result in greater attention to detail and greater results from a direct report, too much fear inflicted on that direct report by their manager can cause increased mistakes, decreased respect, and possibly greater turnover overall on that leader's team.

Regularly explore your intentions for what you want the outcome to be of every conversation you have as a professional. This can help you understand how to best approach each conversation in a way that can prove to be effective and fruitful (as much as possible) for everyone involved.

Tone and psychological safety on teams

Several corporations and nonprofits have reached out to my firm to help their teams communicate as effectively as possible. Especially with some teams working in a hybrid or virtual environment, the ability for teams to engage with one another cohesively has been critical.

My firm was once called on to facilitate training for a small team working in a hybrid format. I was told that on this team, managers and direct reports could use some additional support for both giving feedback to one another and for receiving feedback. Generally, when giving and receiving feedback is a challenge for teams, certain team members' feelings might be hurt by the feedback they receive, and certain managers may be hesitant to provide feedback. The outcome of this can be that team members are both not giving important feedback that could create more impact within the organization and not receiving important feedback that could contribute to both direct reports and managers truly operating as efficiently and effectively as possible in their roles.

In this specific case, my firm conducted a training in which we used assessments to explore the different personality styles of team members to understand what tone and communication approach worked best for each team member, debriefed those assessments so each team member understood their personality and work styles, and then utilized interactive activities and discussion to provide members with practice for using various approaches to communicate effectively with their team members with team members' personality styles in mind.

Team members realized their tone was as important (if not more important) as their words. They also realized that word choice affects the listener, making the listener feel like the tone of the person giving feedback is respectful and professional, resulting in increased trust and built connections. Another realization from the team was that when the tone of delivery is not appropriate for the listener to receive feedback well, that results in more significant conflict and distrust within the team. Team members were super excited by the end of our initial training session and had already started utilizing what they had gained from our training session even before the end of our session!

Even outside of a team training format, you as an individual and especially as a leader at work, can enhance your reputation and contribute significantly to your team's dynamic by taking your tone to the next level when it comes to communication.

What you can do right now

Every day, you have the opportunity to have conversations that create specific outcomes with colleagues. Most likely, you're making different asks, providing feedback, or providing direction as part of those conversations. Here are a few things to do to analyze your tone and shift direction regarding your current approach if needed.

- **Identify key stakeholders for you professionally.** Based on the work you do, create a list of the stakeholders who are key to the outcomes you hope to produce in your role.

- **Rate your tone with key stakeholders.** Reflect on the effectiveness of your tone when it comes to producing desired outcomes with others, how likely it is that your tone exudes confidence, creates more connection and collaboration than conflict, and how your tone is respected (and not feared–there's a difference). On a scale of 1 - 10, rate your tone professionally when it comes to effectiveness, confidence, collaboration, and respect, with 10 being your tone positively influences effectiveness, confidence, collaboration, and respect, and 1 being that your tone very negatively influences effectiveness, confidence, collaboration, and respect. Check out a worksheet you can use to rate your tone with your key stakeholders at www.becomingtheripple.com.

- **Take it up a notch.** Identify the 3 top action steps you can take to take your tone with key stakeholders up one notch on average for the majority of key stakeholders. In other words, identify 3 things you could do that impact your tone overall in a way that affects your life both professionally and personally.

- **Develop a plan.** Once you have identified your top 3 action steps, determine when and in what circumstances you can implement those top action steps. Use a calendar, reminder, or other planning tool to ensure you implement your plan regularly to enhance your tone.

- **Evaluate.** At least 30 days after implementation, go through this process again to evaluate how you now feel about your tone with key stakeholders.

How you communicate with others influences the kind of ripple effect you create as you are becoming the ripple. If you think about some of your most challenging relationships or work environments, then you know that ripple effects are not always positive. In you becoming the ripple, analyzing your tone is key. Taking the time to be intentional about seeing where you are and where you want to be when it comes to tone is critical to elevating your influence and impact on others. As you work more and more to enhance your tone, my hope is that you should see a shift in your professional relationships and opportunities because you are more laser-focused on effectiveness, confidence, collaboration, and respect with your colleagues.

PART IV

YOUR ENVIRONMENT

CHAPTER 10

Be a Culture Changer

"The secret of success is to do the common things uncommonly well."
– John D. Rockefeller

Have you noticed that in most workplaces, a few people stand out as essential to an organization? Let's call them "culture changers." People often want to be on the team of culture changers, or in some cases, even if a culture changer has high expectations for their teams, managers know culture changers get things done. Culture changers in some workplaces may be the individuals who truly define that workplace as having an energetic, driven, or inclusive culture. When a culture changer has transitioned from a team, their absence is felt. Similarly, when a culture changer is on your team, you can feel it too.

If you want to create a substantial impact and influence in your workplace, consider being even more of a culture changer in your professional world. This happens through truly being intentional around your voice as a leader and acknowledging the impact that your voice has. In the book, Crucial Conversations: Tools for Talking When the Stakes Are High, the authors share that individuals who can have difficult, yet essential conversations with anyone–no matter what the seniority or personality style of that person is–are often some of the most successful people in their workplace, regardless of where they work or what they do. There is power in being able to shift the dynamic, direction, and culture of a workplace. Culture changers do that every day.

Why become a culture changer?

Whether you currently don't feel like you're a culture changer professionally or feel like you are a culture changer but could further expand your impact and influence as a culture changer, there are so many reasons to strive to have more influence and more impact at work. Here are a few:

- **More opportunities.** If it's known that you can contribute significantly to any project, you're likely to get additional projects that you might be interested in at work.

- **More professional mentors and sponsors.** In this case, I'll define mentors as individuals who might guide you and provide valuable insights. I'll define sponsors as individuals who might provide you with meaningful financial or other professional opportunities as they advocate for you. Being a culture changer at work can motivate mentors and sponsors to support you further based on their strong belief in your success and potential for greater success. For some of my firm's most successful leadership development clients, their relationships with their mentors and sponsors were key to their professional success.

- **More career growth.** Being a culture changer can result in your career evolving further as you're placed on teams and in rooms, roles, and organizations that your contributions can impact. The teams and companies you work with can also experience growth (and even massive growth in some cases) due to your approach to your work. Being known as a culture changer opens the door for countless opportunities and networks that can provide limitless possibilities for the impact you can make in the world.

Put yourself in the shoes of someone looking to work with you as a culture changer. Of course, most individuals would want to engage with someone who can create an impact in this way. This is why it's essential to consider expanding your influence and impact at work through what you're contributing to your work environment.

Why expand your impact if you're already a culture changer?

Denise came to my firm for leadership development support as she was working in a senior-level role and on the brink of possibly attaining a Chief Executive Officer role within the company. This was a huge move, but for Denise, expanding her impact within her company was a natural fit. Denise already had an established personal brand as an expert in the topics she was passionate about. She traveled the country as an expert panelist and speaker on topics that also lent themselves to enhancing the company's brand. She had already established her brand within her company as a culture changer, practically impacting several systems and approaches that created a long-standing impact on her organization. When she came to my firm, she was ready to create a greater impact, hopeful that she would become a Chief Executive Officer within her organization based on her colleagues' and manager's perspectives on her leadership trajectory.

Denise and I worked on what she would need to have in place to shift into the mindset, personal routines, systems for managing time efficiently, and strategic alliances she would need to cultivate as a Chief Executive Officer. As we worked on these things together, Denise attained her desired Chief Executive Officer role.

One of the things we implemented while she was in her new role was golden hours, an idea whose origin is not well-documented, but that was key for my client to thrive. The concept of having golden hours is that, as a leader, there are major strategic priorities a leader must address even amid actions that a CEO can take that are less urgent and less valuable when it comes to time. For Denise to be able to take care of her organization's most critical priorities, she needed to make time to cultivate relationships with key stakeholders and take necessary follow-up action steps from her frequent meetings. In this role, not only was Denise expanding her impact, but she had additional pressure from key stakeholders to produce results within her role. Here, golden hours were essential for her to calibrate and focus on what was necessary to significantly impact her role. Denise's mission was accomplished. She developed an even greater brand as a results-driven leader within her organization, not only because of her role, but also because of her ability to influence valuable change and growth. For her, expanding her impact as a culture changer meant expanding her brand as an expert, expanding partnerships and collaborations, growing her personal and professional network, and identifying valuable opportunities, all toward a more significant impact on Denise's organization. Denise knew that though she was a culture changer already, her impact could be exponentially greater if she expanded her impact as a culture changer. And that she did.

How does someone become a culture changer?

You may be wondering if culture changers are born or made. Some culture changers have always been able to profoundly impact and influence people around them, despite challenging circumstances. Others have grown into this role. At my firm, I have had the opportunity to observe countless individuals identify where they felt they wanted to enhance their skill sets to have more impact and influence at work and then implement the things that are most important for them to do just that. It's *certainly possible* to either become a culture changer or to become more of one. Here's what usually happens in this process of evolving into more of a culture changer.

Step 1: An event or inspiration. Something happens for you to decide that you want to take your contributions to your work to the next level. You may have received a promotion. Perhaps you're desiring a promotion. Perhaps a circumstance emotionally or spiritually drives you to show up differently. Maybe someone else–a mentor, manager, colleague, friend, or even a family member–has encouraged you to take your contributions to the next level. Maybe you read a book or attended a conference that helped you greatly realize the impact you'd like to make in the workplace.

Step 2: A desire to create a plan. Once someone has made the decision to become a culture changer or to expand their role as a culture changer, they usually try to identify where to start increasing their impact. This plan may include identifying different platforms where this person can be seen more as a culture changer (i.e. meetings, LinkedIn, networking, involvement in corporate initiatives, etc.). Every platform should have its own plan. Consider creating your plan with the advice and guidance of trusted advisors, who might include mentors, sponsors, therapists, coaches, colleagues, or anyone else who could positively influence your pursuit of expanding your impact at work.

Step 3: An implementation of a plan. Any effective plan to enhance your reputation and impact should have a timeline along with milestones. Be sure to celebrate milestones to add to the momentum of accomplishing your plan. Incorporate check-in points monthly or quarterly to identify where you have already been a culture changer professionally and where you might like to expand your reputation and influence towards enhancing your impact at work.

What you can do right now

If you hope to expand your influence and impact professionally, here are a few things you might consider doing:

- **Create a list of ideal examples.** Have you ever heard the term "Success leaves tracks?" Research and create a list of at least 5 individuals you would consider to be culture changers who have career trajectories similar to what you would desire to have. Identify your top 10 key takeaways from your research regarding what actions you may want to consider to expand your impact professionally for whatever that means to you.

- **Create a list of key stakeholders.** Identify the mentors, sponsors, and colleagues you would like to be a part of your career growth. Consider adding a coach, therapist, and other roles to your key stakeholder list who you think might provide additional insights or accountability.

- **Create a list of platforms.** Reflect and document at least 5 platforms you should utilize to enhance your influence and impact. Examples of platforms include 1:1 check-ins with your manager, team meetings, LinkedIn, weekly networking events, media recognition, and more.

- **Create a 90-day, 6-month, and 1-year plan.** Identify the top 3 action steps you would like to take over the next 90 days, 6 months, and 1 year that would increase your influence and impact. Integrate touchpoints with the key stakeholders you defined into your plan as well. Also include monthly or quarterly time to reflect on your accomplishments, where you would like to shift your plan, and what your next priorities are.

Becoming the ripple and being a culture changer are truly synonymous. Chances are, if you are consistently and strategically laser-focused on increasing your influence and your impact towards becoming a culture changer professionally, you will undoubtedly move closer and closer to where you want to be when it comes to the impact you want to have on your life, your company, and who you've been called to be in this world.

CHAPTER 11

Implement the "One-thing" Principle

"The most important thing is to focus on the essential, and not to be distracted by the inessential." – Immanuel Kant

Edith, a franchise owner, was utilizing our firm's consulting services to identify how to increase sales within her service-based business in Tennessee. She had over 20 staff members and her client base had been growing steadily and growth was beginning to slow down. Additionally, she realized that as the owner and operator of her franchise location, she wasn't experiencing as much work-life balance as she would like. She desired her sales to increase. She wanted her staff to thrive. She also wanted to spend more time at home with her husband and children. We brainstormed about solutions to this challenge.

We thought about what the one thing would be that would shift her business operations, sales, and outputs to create the impact she desired. What we came up with was that finding someone talented in sales, who could also be a phenomenal manager, and who had a background in service-based sales would be transformative for Edith and her business.

Edith realized the "one thing" that would shift her business most was filling this specific role–an associate director position. Edith found an individual who was precisely what she was looking for–Farah. Customers loved Farah.

Farah was personable and great at getting new customers and transitioning them to repeat customers. Farah was passionate about ensuring team members felt acknowledged and valued while holding them accountable to high expectations. Farah was also proactive around prospective operations challenges and opportunities. As a result of Farah's contributions to Edith's business, not only did Edith experience increased sales, but she was able to cut the hours she was at her franchise location in half. And there were other unforeseen results as well. Edith hiring Farah created a ripple effect. As a result of having an employee who was such a culture changer, even when other staff members could no longer work in their roles, Farah was flexible enough to keep operations running smoothly–a role that Edith usually would have had to take on.

In this example, Edith expanded her impact as a culture changer by focusing on the "one thing" that would make the most significant difference at her company. Through doing this, Edit was becoming the ripple. But Farah was also a culture changer Edith hired, who was transformative at Edith's company. Farah just so happened to be looking for an opportunity that fit what Edith was looking for at the time based on her life circumstances and desires shifting right around the time that Edith was looking for someone like Farah. For you, there is one thing that could shift your career trajectory, your team's results, or your company's impact. It's essential to periodically reflect on what that one thing might be. Identifying this can be transformative for you and everyone around you, allowing you to be becoming the ripple within your organization.

What happens when you don't have the "one thing"?

If you've ever been on a team where you feel you or your team are taking a lot of action but not moving forward, it's absolutely not a good feeling. You know deep down inside that the actions you all are taking are not producing the right results. Or you might feel like you're all moving towards different goals and that your actions are never enough. Issues with productivity and results on teams and in companies can happen when there is insufficient focus on the top strategic goals that are most important for the team or company.

Having three primary strategic goals is phenomenal. And to scale down even further, having one most important, most valuable initiative, goal, or action step that could be transformative for a company is how you create significant change most efficiently and effectively. It allows everyone to be more aligned on what direction your organization is moving in and what defines success.

Maybe your one thing in your role as an HR executive is to hire a top-performing training and development team. Or maybe your one thing as a marketing leader is to double engagement on your next campaign. Maybe your one thing as a franchise owner is to support your sales team in hitting their sales goals this quarter. Maybe your one thing as an operations executive is to reduce the time taken to implement specific production processes for your team by at least 10%. The results of any of the above initiatives could shift the trajectory of a team or organization and position leaders to be culture changers within their organization. Regularly reflecting on and implementing one significant priority you could drive forward for your organization can create a far-reaching impact now and in the future.

What you can do right now

To reflect on your one thing, you'll implement steps similar to those you did in the rule of 3s section of this book, and you'll also take a few additional action steps to drill down your one thing further.

- **List your key areas.** List the areas of your work that are the key components of what you do.

- **List your priorities.** List the top 5-10 priorities for each area.

- **Hone in your top priorities.** Then, identify the top 3 priorities under each area.

- **Identify your goals.** Reflect on your complete list and identify the top 3 overall goals that would create the most significant impact you're looking for in your role. If you work for an organization where your manager's perception of priorities is different than yours, consider what would make the most impact considering your manager's perspectives as well.

- **Hone in on your top goals.** Then, after you have your top 3 goals overall, take time to reflect on if there is a goal you've identified that is the most significant, most valuable goal that would create the most impact. Or maybe, instead of choosing one of your top 3 goals, you can identify 1 essential action step you should take based on your top 3 goals, that would create the most impact within your organization.

- **Create your plan.** Once you have that 1 thing identified, you'll create a plan to implement it, identifying what you need to do, how you need to do it, and when you need to do it.

Sometimes less is more when it comes to becoming the ripple. Identifying your "one thing" can allow you to be one action away (or even one hire away in Edith's case) from creating a major impact within your organization. Remember that implementing your plan associated with your one thing should indeed create an impact for your team or organization. Though, it will also position you as a culture changer within your company who knows how to create transformative change and who takes action to push change forward in a thoughtful way as well.

CHAPTER 12

Be the Change You Want to See

"You must be the change you wish to see in the world."
– Mahatma Gandhi

At the point of writing this book, I have personally provided individual, group, and team coaching for over 3600 hours for more than ten years. I have learned that there is so much that I gained from my coach training that is directly relevant to leadership development and team development clients. One of those things I learned in coaching training is that your thoughts turn into your feelings, and those feelings turn into your actions. When I first learned this more than ten years ago, I can remember my coaching certification trainer writing on a whiteboard:

Thoughts → Feelings → Actions

Here's an example of how this framework might play out. Let's say that you operate as a senior manager on the research and development team at a Fortune 100 technology firm. One day, the director of research and development comes into your office and shares that the company is rolling out a new project that will impact the user experience for 2 million users. The director shares that she feels you would be best to create the project plan to roll out this new project and that she also feels you would be best to present it to the senior vice presidents at the company during their monthly meeting.

She assures you that even though you haven't facilitated a presentation in front of the senior vice presidents before, she is confident you'll be able to do this effectively based on who you are.

She shares, "You've been to several of these monthly meetings and have seen me share project plans for major projects before. I know you can do this. Feel free to let me know if you have any questions along the way. You'll have two months to prepare before presenting your project plan."

In this example, how might you feel initially in response to this example? What would your first thoughts be about your manager giving you a project they would usually do? After your initial thoughts, what might be the next set of thoughts you might have? Would you go into problem-solving and planning mode? And would you do that with anxious but excited energy or begrudgingly? Would you then procrastinate on your action steps, and be three steps ahead of where your manager thought you might be (time permitting) when it comes to the project? Would you then present your project plan confidently and in a way that could establish your reputation for years to come with senior vice presidents there, or do otherwise?

Let's go through a prospective thought process for one individual in this example using the Thoughts → Feelings → Actions framework. Let's say that Mark is the senior manager. After receiving this project, his **thoughts** are that this is his director's job, and he does not want to be embarrassed. He might also be thinking that the director is just trying to decrease her capacity and that he is already overwhelmed with his workload.

These thoughts may lead to **feelings** like resentment, anxiety, and helplessness. And the **actions** that might come as a result are that even though Mark works diligently on the project, he does not feel like he can ask questions to his manager, the director. He thinks that since he might be embarrassed by the senior vice presidents' perception of him, he doesn't want to risk asking questions to his manager that he doesn't know the answer to. He doesn't want her perception of him to be that he doesn't know his stuff. Consequently, because Mark thinks the director is unfairly giving him too much work and doesn't have his best interest in mind, he also does not want to ask for more time or for his workload to be adjusted for this project, so he's working 80-hour work weeks without asking for additional help from his own direct reports.

As a result of Mark's thoughts, feelings, and actions, he does a good presentation. However, there are pieces of his presentation that could have been much better if he managed up better to attain more guidance and context and if he utilized his direct reports, who had additional capacity, to adjust his workload to be able to focus more on the project. Additionally, his relationship with his director has suffered to an extent because of the resentment he had for her, which she had no idea that he had. The senior vice presidents are still impressed with Mark's presentation but believe he could use more time to grow and develop before his next promotion.

Now, let's go through an example of when the Thoughts → Feelings → Actions framework could be used in a way that produces better results. Let's imagine that Ellen is the senior manager. Her initial **thought** is surprise and a question of whether this project plan and presentation is within her realm of expertise. But then, after her director's encouragement and reinforcement, she believes that this is definitely a project she can take on and implement successfully. She reminds herself of other projects she's taken on that were a challenge for her and realizes that she was able to exceed expectations over and over again despite initially not knowing how to do a project. She reminds herself of what she has done to be able to do that in the past. She also realizes this project can be extremely valuable to Ellen's career trajectory. If she's able to have this platform to engage with senior vice presidents in a way where they can see her expertise and talents in action, that can set her up for an even better annual evaluation from her director and possible opportunities throughout her company in the future.

Ellen's **feelings** as a result of her thoughts are that she is both anxious and excited about this project. She feels blessed to have this opportunity when it could have been given to other colleagues. She already feels proud of herself for taking this project on and is hopeful for a positive outcome for the project. She feels a strong sense of caution balanced with confidence around the project's outcome, knowing the details matter in this project but that it's doable. She also feels supported by her director's belief in her.

As a result of Ellen's feelings, her **actions** are that in her initial meeting with her director when she learns about the project, she shares with her director that she is grateful for this opportunity and for her director's belief in her. Ellen reassures her director that she will do her absolute best to represent her department well regarding this project. After asking some additional questions about the prospective scope of the project in that initial meeting, Ellen also initiates a discussion about readjusting timelines for other projects that may not be as much of a priority to their department. Her director is amenable to those changes. Ellen also asks if a portion of their upcoming check-ins can be dedicated to questions Ellen has that are associated with this project and asks if it's possible to extend check-ins if needed after Ellen starts the project. Her director shares that she is definitely open to that.

After meeting with her director, Ellen also identifies how to redistribute some of the work associated with other projects she's working on to direct reports with additional capacity. She is transparent with those direct reports, sharing about her new project she's been asked to work on, and sharing with her direct reports that she considers a portion of the additional projects she's sharing with them as growth opportunities for direct reports she feels are high potential team members. She ensures that at least a portion of the additional work she is giving them aligns with areas for growth or areas of strength for her direct reports. Ellen's messaging to her direct reports about her belief in them and desire to see them grow gets her direct reports bought into the additional projects they're working on and allows them to see these projects as growth opportunities.

Ellen ends up doing an amazing presentation. She has incorporated best practices for this project's rollout by exploring case studies from similar projects within similar companies. She has tapped into mentors, leaders, and colleagues within the company, who could provide more context, feedback, and research. She honed the presentation with her director, asking for feedback regularly along the way on her progress. She also learned more about the senior vice presidents that she would be speaking to to ensure her presentation exceeded all of their expectations.

The result was that Ellen's annual evaluation from her director was outstanding, positioning her for a bonus and promotion. Two of the senior vice presidents asked to start meeting regularly with Ellen, seeing her as a high-potential team member who could be rising within the ranks of their company. Through her professional connection with those senior vice presidents, little did she know, years later, Ellen would also be sitting in one of their seats as a senior vice president within her company as well.

Mark and Ellen's stories illustrate that if you desire to be in certain roles or be perceived in certain ways professionally, you must focus on what you are thinking about the opportunities and challenges that have come your way. You must address what you might be thinking about your potential and possibilities because, indeed, our thoughts turn into our feelings and our feelings turn into our actions. You should identify who you want to be and how you want to appear in the world. However, working backward to focus on your thoughts and mindset can help you get further faster.

Why be the change you want to see

There's a reason you're reading this book. Maybe it's that you want to create a bigger impact professionally. Perhaps it's that you'd like to move further faster in your current role or that you'd like to move further faster when it comes to attaining higher-level roles. Maybe you're trying to leave a significant mark on your team, on your company, on your community, or on your family.

In order to do this, periodically, it's an extremely powerful and valuable exercise to reflect on and visualize who you aspire to be and then to work towards that. One research study conducted at the University of California, Los Angeles (UCLA) found that individuals who visualized successfully completing the action steps associated with their goals were more likely to take those associated with them. This study also showed that those who visualized action steps tended to be more successful in achieving their goals versus those who only visualized the outcomes.[9] Some articles state that visualization may contribute well to goal achievement because it prepares your mind to be subconsciously more prepared to pursue success by increasing your subconscious belief that you can actually bring your goals to fruition. This greater subconscious belief can result in greater conscious efforts to achieve your goals.

Whatever you hope to do, be very aware of what you must embody on your journey to bring that end goal to fruition. Your heightened awareness and commitment to your end goal should bring you closer to your most desired goals.

---

[9] Pham, L. B., & Taylor, S. E. "From Thought to Action: Effects of Process-Versus Outcome-Based Mental Simulations on Performance." *Personality and Social Psychology Bulletin*, vol. 25, no. 2, 1999, pp. 250-260.

What you can do right now

No matter what you have done or who you have been in the past, you always have the opportunity to embody more of who you aspire to be. Every day is a new opportunity to do so. Here's what you can do to practically be more of who you aspire to be to do more of what you aspire to do:

- **Learn from the past.** Take time to reflect on where you have had challenges or opportunities you feel you haven't responded effectively to in the past 3-6 months. Write down the top 3 "past approaches" that got in the way of you being as effective in your response.

- **Identify new paths forward.** For each of the top 3 things you feel got in the way of you responding effectively to challenges or opportunities in the past, identify 3 "new approaches" that are new statements. Each of your "new approaches" statements would identify a new path forward that is different from each of your "past approaches" statements.
    - For example, if one of your "past approaches" statements is: Instead of volunteering to lead the expansion initiative at work, I was too afraid and missed an opportunity to exhibit my leadership skills, your "new approaches" statement for that specific circumstance might be, "I will fearlessly and expeditiously volunteer for projects that I can lead to exhibit my leadership skills if I am even 70% sure that I have the capacity and expertise to lead the project. Everything is figureoutable, and I will operate with excellence given any challenge."

- **Make the future visible.** Place your 3 new approaches somewhere visible so that you are ready to embody what you aspire to embody when challenges or opportunities arise. Also, incorporate a daily practice of visualizing action steps that lead to the outcomes you most desire. This visualization can also include visualizing you successfully accomplishing your new approaches statements.

If you reflect on the past, maybe you'll see remnants of the kinds of ripples you have created personally and professionally in the past. As you are in the state of becoming the ripple, know that you always have the opportunity to shift the kind of ripple effect you have in the future. My hopes for you are that as you learn from the past, identify new paths forward, and make the future visible, you'll be able to come back to this process whenever you need it to continuously embody more and more of who you aspire to be.

PART V

YOUR SPECIAL TOUCH

CHAPTER 13

Identify Your Special Sauce

"We are what we repeatedly do. Excellence, then, is not an act, but a habit." – Aristotle

If you've ever been to Washington, D.C., and eaten in one of its takeout restaurants, you've most likely tried mumbo sauce. This sauce is special because it's not ketchup and it's not barbecue sauce, but tastes sweet, sour, and spicy, and can be used to add flavor to so many things. It's a red-orange color and I often get a slight smile from people who have tried this in Washington, D.C. when I speak about it. Many years ago, when I lived in Washington, D.C., it used to be that you couldn't get it anywhere else. It was a truly special recipe with such a unique and memorable flavor.

Each of us has our own special recipe for who we are that encompasses what makes us unique. It's your special sauce. This special sauce is a mix of your unique characteristics that have come as a result of what only you have experienced. And when you can take what you experienced–both good and bad–and use it towards characteristics or values that make you a more effective leader, even those challenging experiences can contribute well to your special sauce. Your special sauce might also embody the positive things that team members, managers, direct reports, or even loved ones might say about you.

Your special sauce may relate to the three keys you explored earlier in this book that you exude when you're at your best. When you know what makes you so unique and valuable, it allows you to no longer compete with others so much as you are striving to be the very best version of yourself, exploring what excellence looks like when it comes to honing in on the special mix of what that looks like.

Your special sauce may have been evident since childhood

Ever since I was a small child, I dreamed of changing the world for good. And I was a creative child. Once, I wanted to create some wings at home so I could fly. I was walking to and from school in the Miami sun and just figured flying would be better, so I went about designing and creating some wings (but then, through further reflection in my mind as a child, decided not to try it–I wonder what could have happened!). I remember creating a chair and paper mache art. The possibilities were endless. So, I applied the same creativity to change the world. There were so many possibilities, I thought as a child.

As a child, I once daydreamed that I would change the world through ending homelessness in my city by creating communities where homeless people could have everything they needed to thrive. I had also thought to myself as a child, maybe something could be done where people could go and paint and do other kinds of work in communities that looked like they were in worse condition than theirs. We could all support each other to thrive. I eventually figured out that I might have to wait until I was a grownup to implement some of my big ideas. I was asked to speak about my dreams and goals to my school of over 400 students in elementary school as the designated "Woman of Tomorrow" for the year, and I shared some of my dreams for changing the world in the future with them. I was inspired by all of the possibilities I had to be of value in the lives of others–all from my imagination. As a child, I thought I might also plant seeds of kindness in other children, adults, and strangers that could help make their lives better in different ways.

This love for caring for people and having ideas for solving problems is at the core of my special sauce. I see endless possibilities for others and know how to create momentum around great ideas because of the stories in my life that have served as building blocks for my core values. Even when I have been in the midst of the worst challenges, personally or professionally, this part of my special sauce has stayed consistent. Former colleagues, direct reports, and even managers of mine, before I transitioned into being a business owner, could tell you about my passion for tapping into the potential of people and their ideas. Being a culture changer has long been a part of who I am and is a significant part of my special sauce.

Have you considered what gifts, talents, or positive approaches to your work have been present for you since childhood? Answering that question for yourself could be the key to unlocking new possibilities for how you show up personally and professionally.

What do you bring to the table?

You bring something unique to the table wherever you go when you're at your best. It's a mix of your core values and what you're most likely passionate about. It might relate to why you were hired in certain roles you've been able to receive over the years or why you've received a promotion or accolades from team members in the past. It would be what might come up if a trusted colleague were to provide a reference call for you for a leadership program as they speak about what unique approach, working style, personality style, or leadership style you bring to the table.

Honing your secret sauce

When you hone your secret sauce, magic happens. Honing your secret sauce is taking the skills you are already good at and making them stronger. What happens when a chef perfects his recipe? The chef's reputation grows. People may want more and more of it. Alternatively, when a chef's secret sauce is consistently not as good, that can lend itself to the chef having an inconsistent reputation. You likely have experienced inconsistent recipes at some of your favorite restaurants possibly. This comes as a result of those restaurants not honing their craft enough.

Daily, we have the opportunity to enhance and develop our secret sauce. A Bruce Lee quote states, "I fear not the man who has practiced 10,000 kicks once, but I fear the man who has practiced one kick 10,000 times." So practice your special sauce. Practice your natural gifts to enhance and develop them. And practice them any chance you get daily.

Practice your gift of speaking.
Practice your gift of writing.
Practice your gift of building teams.
Practice your gift of bringing ideas to fruition.
Practice your gift of recruiting top talent.
Practice your gift of growing your company's revenue.
Practice your gift of closing sales seamlessly.
Practice your gift of improving the customer experience.
Practice your gift of being an inspiring leader.
Practice your gift of developing engaging messaging.

Whatever your gifts are, practice them. Sometimes, we may not believe our special sauce is enough because we've diminished its power. Maybe something someone said to us about our natural gift has us trying to hide it. Some of us have diminished our natural gifts in an effort to emulate someone else's, dimming our own light as a result. It's wonderful to aspire to emulate the greatness in others, but not at the cost of not honing your own strengths and uniqueness in the process. Work on perfecting your own gift even as you strengthen your other areas of growth.

What you can do right now

Take the time to explore your special sauce–your own unique strengths that show up when you're the best version of yourself.

- **Talk to colleagues, family, and friends.** Ask at least 3 current or previous colleagues, 3 family members, and 3 friends to share your unique strengths that you bring to the table personally or professionally.

- **Create a list.** Jot down what people are saying about you and identify the throughline of what people say about you that seems to be a common thread regarding the feedback you're receiving.

- **Hone in on your top 3 ingredients to your special sauce.** Clarify and write out what you feel seems to be the top 3 aspects of who you are. For a list of strengths that might embody what your special sauce could be, check out a categorized list I created at www.becomingtheripple.com.

- **Make your special sauce visible.** Identify how you'll be reminded of your special sauce in the future. You might post a sticky note on your fridge, laptop, or bulletin board with 3 phrases that embody the top 3 ingredients of your special sauce. Or maybe you might have a daily pop-up reminder on your phone reminding you of your special sauce. Find what works for you and implement that moving forward.

- **Remember to hone your special sauce.** One of the most valuable things you can do is to ensure that your special sauce is perfected as much as possible. Since others already recognize it as a natural gift, identify how, when, and where you can hone your special sauce regularly to consistently add to your reputation and results, just as a great special sauce significantly enhances the flavor of any great recipe!

Your special sauce should embody the essence of the kind of ripple effect you hope to have on the world as you are becoming the ripple. Exploring your special sauce can be a truly valuable, eye-opening experience because it forces you to look at yourself, your potential, and your value through other people's eyes. When you discover what your special sauce is, it can create ripples in many different areas of your life, both personally and professionally. Remember to not only embrace your special sauce and acknowledge its value, but also, to hone your special sauce regularly to grow your influence and your impact.

CHAPTER 14

Infuse Your Strengths Into Your Work

"Be sure you put your feet in the right place, then stand firm."
– Abraham Lincoln

In the previous chapter, when referencing your special sauce, I shared how important it is to identify how, when, and where to integrate your special sauce. This idea of infusing your special sauce–your strengths–into your work is such a critically important idea that it deserves its own chapter. Have you ever had a job that you felt just wasn't a great fit, where it wasn't that it was a negative work culture but it just seemed like it wasn't a fit for you? You possibly felt uncomfortable or anxious doing your role. Maybe it seemed like your work dragged on and on. Or perhaps it seemed you made several mistakes you shouldn't have made. Or possibly your direct reports or manager and you seem to be on very different pages. There could be so many different things going on in these cases, but part of the issue in many of those instances could be that you are not yet infusing your strengths into your work as much as you should. Your strengths should be infused into your work just as if you were a chef, your special sauce might be infused into any great recipe.

Finding new ways to infuse your strengths into your work

In some cases, you may pursue a shift in your scope of work or a change in your role at work that might allow you to infuse your strengths into your work. It may be time to have a conversation with your supervisor about taking on more projects or opportunities that might shine a light on your strengths in a way that can impact your growth and development and increase the impact you have on your company. Your supervisor might even have a project they are working on that they might allow you to implement based on the skillsets and strengths you'd like to utilize more.

Reflect on if it might be the case with you that you could create additional opportunities, propose specific opportunities, or even advocate for different opportunities to contribute your strengths to your organization. You'll, of course, continue to hone and master your strengths even as you're infusing them more into your organization.

Examples of successful people who have turned challenges into strengths

I would be remiss if I didn't also point out that for some of you, the challenges and hardships you've experienced prevent you from fully seeing your strengths as realistic. Your challenges might also prevent you from feeling you could truly strive for greatness personally and professionally. If this is you, know that I am so sorry for all you've experienced. I am sorry for your losses and even if we have never met, I genuinely continue to have hope for your future wins. If you feel you could use more hope and belief, you can do several things to increase your level of hope and belief in your potential. One thing that you can do that my past leadership development clients have utilized, even as recently as this past week is to explore stories of others who have overcome challenges, especially if their challenges are similar to yours. You can read, watch, and listen to the stories of others who have successfully overcome their challenges and hardships to inspire and equip you on your journey. Here are a few examples:

Marilyn Hewson: Former Chief Executive Officer of Lockheed Martin

When Marilyn Hewson was only nine years old, her father passed away. Suddenly, Hewson's mother had to raise five children independently and work multiple jobs to keep up with the household's financial needs. As Hewson's family experienced financial struggles during this time, her mother instilled in Hewson the importance of education and hard work. Hewson attended the University of Alabama, working different part-time jobs to pay for college.

She earned a bachelor's degree in business administration and started working at Lockheed Martin in 1983. There, she utilized strengths like perseverance, work ethic, and innovation to rise within the ranks of Lockheed Martin, where she became the CEO in 2013. She was the first woman CEO at Lockheed Martin. Lockheed Martin grew significantly during Hewson's time as CEO and Hewson earned a reputation as an innovative leader and trailblazer in the aerospace and defense industry. Hewson turned her challenges into strengths, using the perseverance, work ethic, and innovation she used in college and while rising in the ranks at Lockheed Martin and eventually becoming CEO at Lockheed Martin. Her strengths were part of her special sauce and she utilized them to make a significant mark on Lockheed Martin in a way that received worldwide attention.[10]

John Paul Jones DeJoria: Co-Founder of John Paul Mitchell Systems and Patron Spirits Company

John Paul Jones DeJoria went from being homeless and in foster care to later becoming a billionaire. He was the child of immigrants from Italy and Greece. As a child, he and his sibling were sent to an East Los Angeles foster home because his single mother wasn't able to support both children. They stayed

---

[10] "Marillyn Hewson Biography, Life & Interesting Facts Revealed." *Learn Biography*, 23 Feb. 2024, https://learnbiography.com/marillyn-hewson/. Accessed 15 Aug. 2024.

in that foster home for a few years. At nine, DeJoria and his older brother started to sell Christmas cards and newspapers to support their family.

Over the years, DeJoria worked in several jobs, including as a janitor, a door-to-door encyclopedia salesman, and an insurance salesman, often using his above-and-beyond work ethic, perseverance, and communication skills to bring in income. In 1980, he and hairdresser Paul Mitchell formed John Paul Paul Mitchell Systems with just $700. This was the same year that marked the last year that he would be homeless. Between co-founding Patron and Paul Mitchell, DeJoria eventually became a billionaire. The same above-and-beyond work ethic, perseverance, and communication skills that John Paul Jones DeJoria used to push past his challenges at a very young age served as a core foundation for him to infuse those same strengths into the work he did later on in life that eventually made him a billionaire.[11][12]

Rosalind Brewer: Former Chief Executive Officer of Walgreens Boots Alliance and Former Chief Executive Officer of Sam's Club

Walgreens Boots Alliance (WBA) operates over 12,500 locations across the U.S., Europe, and Latin America and has over 331,000 team members across eight countries, according to walgreensbootsalliance.com. WBA owns Walgreens in the U.S. and Boots in the UK in addition to other companies. In 2021, Rosalind Brewer became the first woman to become CEO of WBA, having previously served as COO and Group President at Starbucks as well as previously having served as CEO of Sam's Club.

---

[11] "Veteran of the Day: Navy Veteran John Paul DeJoria." *VA News*, U.S. Department of Veterans Affairs, 27 July 2023, https://news.va.gov/116131/veteranoftheday-navy-john-paul-dejoria/#:~:text=John%20Paul%20DeJoria%20was%20born,being%20placed%20in%20foster%20care. Accessed 15 Aug. 2024.

[12] Krier, Beth Ann. "You Can Go from Absolute Zero to Millions, Says Hair-Care Mogul John Paul Jones DeJoria. He's Got the Business and the Toys to Prove It." *Los Angeles Times*, 20 Dec. 1991, https://www.latimes.com/archives/la-xpm-1991-12-20-vw-599-story.html. Accessed 15 Aug. 2024.

Brewer's story is also one of overcoming challenges and utilizing her strengths to be successful. Brewer is the youngest of five children and grew up in Detroit within a family experiencing financial difficulties. Her parents stressed to her the importance of education, and Brewer went on to earn a bachelor's degree in chemistry.[13] Brewer became CEO of WBA at a time when WBA locations were playing an essential role in the rollout of COVID-19 vaccines across the United States. Brewer was key in making sure that operations and systems were in place to ensure safety, equity, and efficiency in the COVID-19 vaccine rollout.[14] She used problem-solving, adversity, and hope to overcome challenges within her various roles–skills that she had to use in her youth to push past any obstacles or barriers she might have faced in her journey.

Do you notice the trend in the stories above? Every individual had some major adversities or challenges they pushed through, and I just shared a portion of their stories. They must have all experienced even more challenges along the way. However, they all identified their special sauce and infused it into their work. They all utilized their strengths to move them forward into the success that they were destined to experience if they continued to move forward.

What you can do right now

In your professional life, are there different places, initiatives, or relationships where you realize you can further infuse your strengths? Here is an exercise

---

[13] "Glass Ceiling Slayer: Roz Brewer Dubs Grads." *Starbucks Stories & News*, Starbucks Corporation, 7 May 2018, stories.starbucks.com/stories/2018/glass-ceiling-slayer-roz-brewer-dubs-grads/. Accessed 15 Aug. 2024.

[14] "Walgreens Boots Alliance Announces Leadership Transition." *Walgreens Boots Alliance*, 1 Mar. 2023, www.walgreensbootsalliance.com/news-media/press-releases/2023/walgreens-boots-alliance-announces-leadership-transition/#:~:text=Roz%20Brewer%20was%20named%20Chief,plan%20to%20drive%20vaccine%20equity. Accessed 15 Aug. 2024.

you can do right now to help you explore the next steps for infusing your strengths more into your work:

- **Reflect on your special sauce.** Go back to where you identified your special sauce earlier and write down what that special sauce is. Be sure to think of your unique strengths that contribute most to your professional success.

- **Make a list.** Create a list of places, initiatives, or relationships where you could infuse your strengths more.

- **Elaborate.** For each place, initiative, or relationship, write one thing you could do practically to infuse your special sauce there. Note which strength you would be infusing through this action. Be sure to write down something you could later measure to see if you have done it. For example, you might write:
    - Coffee chats with coworkers: Learn 1 new thing about my coworker's interests, perspectives, or family to infuse my strength of connection here.

- **Choose your top 3.** Choose 3 components from your list to work on over the next 30 days. And feel free to come back and choose up to three more every month as you continue to further infuse your strengths into your work.

Each ripple you create should have your special sauce infused through it as you are becoming the ripple. You or your colleagues might notice more and more of a shift in how you show up as you take your gifts, talents, and strengths to the next level at work over time. Most importantly, you will grow your influence and impact towards the success you desire over time. Remember, from the stories I shared earlier, your possibilities are truly endless.

CHAPTER 15

Becoming the Ripple: Making W.A.V.E.S.™

"Do not stop thinking of life as an adventure. You have no security unless you can live bravely, excitingly, imaginatively; unless you can choose a challenge instead of competence." – Eleanor Roosevelt

Your life, both personally and professionally, is indeed an adventure. And like the most thrilling adventures, every day provides a fantastic opportunity to practice the art of expanding your impact, allowing you to regularly practice embodying the ripple effect that every company needs.

Companies and organizations need individuals who will not only meet the expectations of their roles, but who understand their **w**hy, who will take strategic **a**ction, who know their **v**oice needs to be one that creates influence, who take their work **e**nvironment to the next level by what they contribute to it, and who are clear on their **s**pecial touch in a way that their strengths are infused into their work. That kind of individual is a leader who not only creates a ripple effect of impact within their companies but is always thinking of ways of constantly becoming the ripple–an active, ongoing commitment to continuously pursue growing their influence and impact wherever they go within their companies.

It is never too late to start embodying what you aspire to be. We are always in a state of becoming, with life's moments always passing away and making space for new moments, new possibilities, and new opportunities.

Becoming the ripple in your everyday life

My ask to you is that you realize the impact of who you are becoming. As I write this, I recently took on a volunteer role within an organization and am focusing very much on supporting the enhancement of culture within the organization. Someone today stopped next to me in her car, rolled down her window, and shouted to me excitedly, "I just wanted to share with you that I think you have the ability to single-handedly transform the culture of this organization and help us to have the greater connection and culture we've needed!" I was taken aback and speechless. I will tell you what I know for sure. I know that I can't do anything on my own. I know that the greatest way I can serve others whether volunteering or in my professional work, is to spark something great in someone else through who I strive to be, how I strive to do my work, what I say, and how I bring others along. This is an ongoing process. It's a process of always becoming, and in this case, becoming the ripple.

The possibilities of your impact are endless as they relate to you becoming the ripple. Becoming the ripple is what you have the opportunity to do every day. Every day, you have the opportunity to influence and impact others in a way that can create lasting change for you and those around you. You can be becoming the ripple for your team. You can be becoming the ripple for your company as a whole. You can be becoming the ripple at a professional event. You can be becoming the ripple for your family.

A real-life example of a world-changer's journey to becoming the ripple

One of my favorite people who I've studied and listened to various interviews about is Maya Angelou. She is such a great example of becoming the ripple and being continually in the process of becoming. As a child, Angelou went through a plethora of challenges. She experienced her parents divorcing and was sent afterward to live with her grandmother in Stamps, Arkansas. As a result of experiencing a traumatic event while there, she was mute for five years, not saying a word to anyone. Some who knew her then would have doubted that she would speak again.

During those years of being mute, Maya Angelou read quite a bit, developing a love for classic literature and the language within the books she read. She began to speak again. As an adult, she later worked alongside Martin Luther King Jr. in the Civil Rights Movement and created volumes of poetry, autobiographies, and essays. As a result of her work, she received the Presidential Medal of Freedom in 2011, among many other awards and honors throughout her life. Though she passed away in 2014, she spent decades mentoring many individuals, fighting for human rights and social justice, and using her voice for good.

We can learn a lot about becoming a ripple from Maya Angelou. We can see that sometimes our greatest gifts and even our special sauce may come from our challenges or times of darkness. You may be great at speaking up at meetings because you may not have felt you had a voice at one point in your life. You may be great at problem-solving because it's how you were able to help yourself and maybe even your family be resourceful. You may be excellent at managing because you may have experienced feeling lost or helpless in a role and don't want others to experience that. Your overcoming has now allowed you to create a positive ripple effect for others.

We can learn from Maya Angelou that you can continue growing, expanding, and impacting no matter what level you currently perceive yourself to be professionally. When I first heard about Maya Angelou in the 1990's, she was already such a star in my eyes. She didn't stop operating in her gift even at her level of success. She expanded and impacted and created more ripples of impact. She expanded more, impacted more, and created more ripples of impact. Even at 82 years old, Maya Angelou was still creating more and more ripples of impact, receiving the Presidential Medal of Freedom at that age. She most likely had to reflect and identify what becoming the ripple would look like at every stage of her life, and just as she had the opportunity to determine what that looked like for her, we also have the opportunity to reflect on what continuously becoming the ripple looks like in our lives.

Why YOU becoming the ripple is what the world is missing

You are the only person in the world born with your unique set of experiences, ideas, vision, and approach. When you operate fully in your gifts and talents and do what you're called to do, it impacts everything around you. Your life is impacted, your teams are impacted, your company is impacted, your family is impacted, your friends are impacted, and history literally changes as a result of you becoming the ripple.

Taking the time to identify what that looks like for you both personally and professionally is well worth your time and can result in dividends you couldn't even imagine.

In fact, when I stop–I mean really stop–and acknowledge everything around me that has happened as a result of when I have chosen to be becoming the ripple, I am grateful. I can see the results every day with my firm, the individuals I have mentored, my home, my family, and even in my hopeful state of mind. I am a dreamer. I am someone who takes action. I am someone who truly believes in others. And even though I, like all of us, can make mistakes at times, I can see that when I choose to operate in the fullest version of myself, everything around me is truly impacted. You might see that in your own life too. And if you haven't yet, that's one of my greatest wishes for you.

Why becoming the ripple is within reach for everyone

All ripples look different. Some are large and wide. Some are small and subtle. Both create impact. You don't have to be the loudest or most prominent person in the room to create the impact that you aspire to create. You don't have to be in a C-suite role, a senior leader, or even a manager to create that impact. However, you do have to be willing to persevere through your challenges, fears, and hesitations to do that which you are called to do. Think about someone at a company you do business with who was not in a senior-level role but provided you with such an amazing experience as a customer that you felt inclined to leave a positive review or were inclined to continuously support this business or nonprofit. Individuals within any role in an organization can create a ripple effect. Will you accept the calling to pursue being all you're meant to be, whether your end goal is more impact for others or for your own life? And will you have the courage to be gracious with yourself when you fall short so that you can continue to move forward in becoming the ripple?

If you're reading this, I know you have all it takes to move forward in greatness in a way that will create a far-reaching impact. You wouldn't have taken the time and made the effort to delve deeper into how to create more success for yourself, your work, and those around you. You are already becoming a ripple. My wish for you is that you continue onward in a spirit of endless possibility as you continuously are becoming more and more of who you aspire to be.

Afterword

"You can never leave footprints that last if you are always walking on tiptoe." – Leymah Gbowee

I sincerely thank you for reading this book. I started to speak on the topics I wrote about in this book during the height of the COVID-19 pandemic in 2020. I would speak about these topics to help people create more connection, productivity, and indeed, resilience amid arguably one of the most challenging times that many have experienced. I did many virtual speeches and training sessions that year and it would give me so much peace to see how individuals and teams would leave my talks, especially that year. Team members and leaders would ask if we could extend our virtual workshops towards the end of the workshop, and I believe it was because there was such a need for the topics I was sharing about. People wanted to feel re-energized and equipped to thrive regardless of their starting place.

Years later, I continue to be asked to facilitate training sessions for teams and leaders about topics I touched on in this book. I believe it's because positive connection, productivity, and reputation are all natural human desires and are crucial to transforming individuals, teams, and organizations. These components are at the core of the highest-performing teams and are aligned with the leadership values of some of the most successful companies today.

So this book is my gift to you. It's one compassionate gesture I'm making to further equip and inspire you to be all you can be so that you are continuously becoming the ripple. Be inspired. Take action. I'm excited about the possibilities of what you continuously becoming the ripple produces in your life and work.

Onwards and upwards,

Daphne Valcin

Made in the USA
Columbia, SC
23 September 2024